First World War
and Army of Occupation
War Diary
France, Belgium and Germany

15 DIVISION
Headquarters, Branches and Services
Royal Army Ordnance Corps
Deputy Assistant Director Ordnance Services
4 July 1915 - 27 June 1919

WO95/1922/1

The Naval & Military Press Ltd
www.nmarchive.com
Published in association with The National Archives

Published by

The Naval & Military Press Ltd

Unit 10 Ridgewood Industrial Park,

Uckfield, East Sussex,

TN22 5QE England

Tel: +44 (0) 1825 749494

www.naval-military-press.com

www.nmarchive.com

This diary has been reprinted in facsimile from the original. Any imperfections are inevitably reproduced and the quality may fall short of modern type and cartographic standards.

© **Crown Copyright**
Images reproduced by permission of The National Archives, London, England, 2015.

Contents

Document type	Place/Title	Date From	Date To
Heading	WO95/1922/1		
Heading	15th Division D.A.D.O.S. Jly 1915-Jun 1919		
Heading	15th Division D.A.D.O.S. XVth Division Vol. I. 4-31.7.15		
Heading	War Diary of D.A.D.O.S. XV Division from 4th July to 31st July 1915		
War Diary	Marlborough	04/07/1915	08/07/1915
War Diary	France.	09/07/1915	31/07/1915
Heading	15th Division Hd: Qrs: 15th Division D.A.D.O.S. Vol: II August 15		
Heading	XV Division War Diary D.A.D.O.S. August 1915		
War Diary	Head Qn XV Division.	01/08/1915	30/08/1915
Heading	War Diary of D.A.D.O.S.-XV Division from 1st September to 30th September 1915		
War Diary	Headquarters XV. Division	03/09/1915	27/09/1915
Heading	15th Division H.Q. 15th Div. D.A.D.O.S. Vol 4 Oct 15		
Heading	War Diary D.A.D.O.S. XV Division October 1915		
War Diary		01/10/1915	29/10/1915
Heading	H.Q. 15th Division D.A.D.O.S. Vol: 5 Nov 15		
Heading	War Diary D.A.D.O.S. XV Division November 1915		
War Diary		03/11/1915	25/11/1915
Heading	D.A.D.O.S. 15th. Div: Vol: 6 December 1915		
War Diary		01/12/1915	31/12/1915
Heading	D.A.D.O.S. 15th Div: Vol. 7		
War Diary	Auchel	02/01/1916	17/01/1916
War Diary	Noeux Les Mines	20/01/1916	30/01/1916
Heading	D.A.D.O.S. 15th Div: Vol: 8		
War Diary	Noeux-Les-Mines	01/02/1916	27/02/1916
Heading	D.A.D.O.S. 15th Div Vol. 9		
War Diary	Noeux-Les-Mines	02/03/1916	27/03/1916
War Diary	Lillers	02/04/1916	27/04/1916
War Diary	Bethune	27/04/1916	30/04/1916
War Diary	Bethune	01/05/1916	31/05/1916
Miscellaneous	D.A.G. 3rd Echelon Bttn 1st July 1916	01/07/1916	01/07/1916
War Diary	Bethune	01/06/1916	30/06/1916
Heading	War Diary July. 1916 Army Ordnance Department D.A.D.O.S. 15th Division		
War Diary	Bethune.	01/07/1916	31/07/1916
Heading	War Diary D.A.D.O.S. 15th Division Period. 1st-31st August 1916 15 D.A.D.O.S. Vol 14		
Heading			
War Diary	Vignacourt	01/08/1916	08/08/1916
War Diary	Albert	14/08/1916	31/08/1916
Heading	Vol 15 War Diary September, 1916 D.A.D.O.S. 15th Divn.		
Miscellaneous	Memorandum		
War Diary	Albert	02/09/1916	20/09/1916
War Diary	Montigny	21/09/1916	23/09/1916
Heading	War Diary October. 1916 D.A.D.O.S. 15th Divn		
War Diary	Montigny	01/10/1916	01/10/1916

War Diary	Albert-Amiens Road.	13/10/1916	15/10/1916
War Diary	Becourt Wood	16/10/1916	29/10/1916
Heading	War Diary November. 1916 D.A.D.O.S. 15th. Divn. Vol 17		
Miscellaneous	Officer Commanding		
Heading	DAA & QMS 15 Div.	30/11/1916	30/11/1916
War Diary	Becourt Wood	02/11/1916	04/11/1916
War Diary	Millencourt.	05/11/1916	06/11/1916
War Diary	Baizieux	12/11/1916	30/11/1916
Heading	War Diary Vol 18 December. 1916 D.A.D.O. 15 Div.		
Miscellaneous	Memorandum		
War Diary	Baizieux.	01/12/1916	03/12/1916
War Diary	Albert	03/12/1916	31/12/1916
Heading	War Diary for Jany 1917 Vol 19 D.A.D.O.S. 15. Div.		
Miscellaneous	Memorandum		
War Diary	Albert	01/01/1917	31/01/1917
Heading	War Diary for February. 1917. D.A.D.O.S. 15th Divn. Vol 20		
War Diary	Albert	01/02/1917	03/02/1917
War Diary	Baizieux	04/02/1917	14/02/1917
War Diary	Beauval Boquemaison	16/02/1917	18/02/1917
War Diary	Roellecourt.	19/02/1917	27/02/1917
Heading	War Diary for March. 1917 D.A.D.O.S. 15 Div.		
War Diary	Roellecourt.	01/03/1917	08/03/1917
War Diary	Duisans	14/03/1917	30/03/1917
Heading	(Original) War Diary April. 1917. D.A.D.O.S. 15 Div Vol 22		
War Diary	Duisans	04/04/1917	21/04/1917
War Diary	War Diary for May. 1917. D.A.D.O.S. 15 Div Vol 23		
War Diary	Duisans	04/05/1917	08/05/1917
War Diary	Le Cauroy.	09/05/1917	22/05/1917
War Diary	Willeman	22/05/1917	26/05/1917
Heading	War Diary June. 1917 DADOS 15 Divn Vol 24		
War Diary	Willeman	01/06/1917	18/06/1917
War Diary	Vlamertinghe	25/06/1917	28/06/1917
Heading	War Diary July DADOS. 15. Divn. Vol 25		
War Diary	Vlamertinghe	06/07/1917	31/07/1917
Heading	DADOS 15. Division War Diary August 1917		
War Diary	Vlamertinghe	03/08/1917	04/08/1917
War Diary	Winnizeele	18/08/1917	18/08/1917
War Diary	Vlamertinghe.	28/08/1917	31/08/1917
Heading	War Diary for September. 1917 DADOS 15. Divn Vol 27		
War Diary	Watou	02/09/1917	05/09/1917
War Diary	Hermaville.	07/09/1917	08/09/1917
War Diary	Arras	09/09/1917	28/09/1917
Heading	War Diary October. 1917. Vol. 1917		
War Diary	Arras.	01/10/1917	31/10/1917
Heading	War Diary. D.A.D.O.S. 15. Division November. 1917.		
War Diary	Arras.	01/11/1917	30/11/1917
Heading	War Diary. December. 1917. D.A.D.O.S. 15th Division. Vol 30		
War Diary	Arras	08/12/1917	27/12/1917
Heading	War Diary of D.A.D.O.S. 15th Division from 1/2/18-To 28/2/18		
War Diary	Arras.	01/02/1918	27/02/1918

Type	Location	From	To
Heading	D.A.D.O.S. 15th Division War Diary. March 1918. Vol 33		
War Diary	Arras	10/03/1918	23/03/1918
War Diary	Warlus	24/03/1918	31/03/1918
Heading	War Diary.-April, 1918. D.A.D.O.S. 15th Division.		
War Diary	Warlus.	02/04/1918	24/04/1918
War Diary	Auchel	26/04/1918	30/04/1918
Heading	War Diary May 1918. D.A.D.O.S. 15th Division.		
War Diary	Auchel.	04/05/1918	04/05/1918
War Diary	Agnez Duisans	05/05/1918	28/05/1918
Heading	War Diary For June, 1918. D.A.D.O.S. 15th Division.		
War Diary	Agnez-Les Duisans	01/06/1918	30/06/1918
Heading	War Diary. D.A.D.O.S. 15th Divn. July. 1918		
War Diary	Agnez Duisans	05/07/1918	14/07/1918
War Diary	Previn-Cadelle.	15/07/1918	16/07/1918
War Diary	Bryas	17/07/1918	18/07/1918
War Diary	Liancourt.	19/07/1918	19/07/1918
War Diary	Pierrefonds	20/07/1918	20/07/1918
War Diary	Guise La Motte	22/07/1918	22/07/1918
War Diary	Vivieres	23/07/1918	29/07/1918
Heading	War Diary. August 1918 DADOS. 15th Divn.		
War Diary	Vivieres	01/08/1918	04/08/1918
War Diary	Liancourt	06/08/1918	06/08/1918
War Diary	Ambrines	08/08/1918	16/08/1918
War Diary	Montenescourt	18/08/1918	25/08/1918
War Diary	Braquemont.	26/08/1918	31/08/1918
Heading	War Diary for September 1918 D.A.D.O.S. 15 Division Vol 39		
War Diary	Braquemont.	01/09/1918	26/09/1918
Heading	War Diary October. 1918. DADOS. 15th Division. Vol 40		
War Diary	Braquemont	06/10/1918	18/10/1918
War Diary	Carvin	19/10/1918	19/10/1918
War Diary	Thumeries	20/10/1918	20/10/1918
War Diary	Capelle	20/10/1918	21/10/1918
War Diary	Genech.	23/10/1918	25/10/1918
War Diary	La Glanerie.	26/10/1918	26/10/1918
Heading	War Diary of D.A.D.O.S. 15th (Scottish) Division. From November 1st 1918. To November 30th. 1918. Vol 41		
War Diary	La Glanerie. Wez. Antoing Tourpes	02/11/1918	17/11/1918
War Diary	Ormeignies	18/11/1918	30/11/1918
Heading	War Diary D.A.D.O.S. 15th Division Period:- Dec: 1st 1918 to Dec: 31st 1918		
War Diary	Ormeignies	03/12/1918	16/12/1918
War Diary	Braine Le Chateau	20/12/1918	31/12/1918
Heading	War Diary. D.A.D.O.S. 15th. Division Period Jan 1st-31st, 1919. Vol		
Miscellaneous	Memorandum		
War Diary	Braine Le Chateau	01/01/1919	31/01/1919
Heading	War Diary D.A.D.O.S. 15th. Division February, 1919		
War Diary	Braine-Le-Chateau	05/02/1919	06/02/1919
War Diary	Tubize U.K.	14/02/1919	19/02/1919
War Diary	Braine-Le-Chateau	20/02/1919	27/02/1919
Heading	Vol 45 War Diary D.A.D.O.S., 15th Division. March. 1919.		

War Diary	Brain-Le-Chateau	01/03/1919	28/03/1919
War Diary	Clabecq	28/03/1919	28/03/1919
War Diary	Brain-Le Comte	28/03/1919	28/03/1919
Heading	D.A.D.O.S. 15th Division War Diary For March 1919		
Heading	War Diary D.A.D.O.S., 15th Division. April, 1919.		
War Diary	Braine Le Chateau	02/04/1919	02/04/1919
War Diary	Braine Le Comte	03/04/1919	11/04/1919
War Diary	Tubize	16/04/1919	16/04/1919
War Diary	Clabecq	17/04/1919	17/04/1919
War Diary	Inbize	22/04/1919	22/04/1919
War Diary	Hal.	01/05/1919	27/06/1919

WO 95/1922 (1)

15TH DIVISION

D. A. D.O.S.

JLY 1915 - JUN 1919

15th Division

S.A.D.O.S. XVth Division
Vol. I. 4 — 31.7.15.

June '19

11/696

Confidential

WAR DIARY

of

D.A.D.O.S. XV DIVISION

from 4th July to 31st July 1915

WAR DIARY / INTELLIGENCE SUMMARY

D.A.D.O.S. XI DIVISION

Army Form C. 2118

Month: July 1915

Place	Date	Hour	Summary of Events and Information	Remarks and references to Appendices
Marlboro'	4th	1.15 am	Orders received for embarkation of the Division and lists of shoes deficient sent to 37th division as ordered by W.O. local letter.	
"	5th	—	} Preparing for embarkation i.e. Completing units with W.D. equipment.	
"	6th	—	}	
"	7th	—	}	
—	8th	Mid night	Embarked at FOLKESTONE.	
France	9th	3.30 am	Arrived at BOULOGNE and proceeded North at 10 AM	
"	"	3 PM	Arrived at TILQUES via ST. OMER. Railhead ST. OMER.	
"	10th	Noon	Reported arrival to DDOS. GHQ	
"	11th	—	Received instructions from Ordnance Communications to indent on HAVRE	
"	13th	—	12000 Smoke helmets received and issued.	
"	14th	—	Received WO letter No 121/54/18 dated 28/6/15 approving of the addition of 3 Wagons G.S. and 2 Wagons limbered GS	
"	15th	—	"Implements Ammunition Keys No 12 Mark II Setting No 80 and 83 fuzes" in possession of RFA Batteries reported as not fitting the No 85 fuze; and were withdrawn for alteration Wooley.	
"	15	7AM	Division marched to RENESCURE arrived Noon and bivouacked.	
"	16	"	Division " to BOURECQ " " "	
"	17	"	Division " to GOSNAY " " into Billets	
"	18	—	Railhead THIENNES, and refilling point (2) fixed. 7500 Smoke helmets received and issued. Received instructions to withdraw rifles from Artillery units Ammunition Column, Divisional Train & Field Ambulance.	

Army Form C. 2118

DADOS. XVDIVISION (folio 2)

WAR DIARY / INTELLIGENCE SUMMARY

July 1915 (Continued)

Instructions regarding War Diaries and Intelligence Summaries are contained in F.S. Regs., Part II. and the Staff Manual respectively. Title Pages will be prepared in manuscript.

(Erase heading not required.)

Place	Date	Hour	Summary of Events and Information	Remarks and references to Appendices
France.	19"	-	4125 Smoke helmets received and issued. Received notification of the division.	
	20	-	Received W.O. Letta. 121/8104/2865 of 14.7.15. 20: Withdrawal of 3 airman team @ Judgs from infantry units.	
	22	-	Visited by DD.O.S. 1st Army. Received orders to withdraw 3 airman range finders from the Pioneer battalion. 13 additional LEWIS machine guns received and issued to battalions (making a total of 4 machine guns each)	
	23	-	Received orders from DD.O.S. 1st Army to withdraw rifles from Supply Column and M.T. Cav drivers. Divisional Head Quarters	
	24	-	Certain Stores in possession of Pioneer battalion withdrawn under authority of War Office Letter 79/7628 (S.D.2) dated 9.6.15.	
	25	-	Received instructions that orders had been given to Glengarry Caps to be exchanged for Balmoral Bonnets.	
	26	-	Received notification that demands for waterproof bags to replace Khaki drill Caps should be formed	
	27	-	Consolidated demand for waterproof bags forwarded	
	28	-	Received L.D. memo. Q.M.G./9/B/3055 dated 22.7.15 re: Spare parts for LEWIS machine guns.	
	29	-	Demanded 1 G.S. Wagon (complete limbered) for divisional Ammunition Column (for M.Th. machine gun battery. authority. Q.M.G. No. 9/2911 of G.H.Q. 26/c/s A.Q.M.G. 4. Corps 27.7.15.	

DADOS. XI DIVISION

WAR DIARY or **INTELLIGENCE SUMMARY** July 1915 (concluded)

Folio 3

Army Form C. 2118

Place	Date	Hour	Summary of Events and Information	Remarks and references to Appendices
France	31st	—	Last battalion issued with Tan. O'Shanters - all units now equipped. Received order to withdraw all S.E. rifles, long & short from Clerks, Officers servants, grooms etc. etc. auth'y DDOS 1st Army O.S. 7/52/1 dated 29.7.15. F Smith Major DADOS XI Division 31.7.15	

121/6753

15th Division

KASOS

MS. Op: 15th Division
Vol: II

August 15

XV DIVISION

WAR DIARY D.A.D.O.S.

August 1915

WAR DIARY or INTELLIGENCE SUMMARY

Army Form C. 2118

XI Division

August 1915

Place	Date	Hour	Summary of Events and Information	Remarks and references to Appendices
Head Qr XI Divsn	August 1	-	Rec. O.S.G/5798/446 introducing the pocket to smoke helmet to be sewn into left skirt of jacket, also D.O.S. O.G/5951/446 dated 31/7/15 directing provision of a satchel for carrying 2nd smoke helmet.	7 May
				15 May
			Report sent to DDOS 1st Army re: unsatisfactory method of packing tomoine sprayers in transport.	15 May
	5	-	O.S./45/90 4/8/15 directing that 20% of the Reserve of smoke helmets should be held by units provided storage is available.	15 May
	6	-	165 steel helmets allotted to XI Dn. for trial. 4th Corps 4688(A) 4/8	15 May
	8	-	GHQ. 317. O.S/48/90/12 5/8/15 Instructions re: issue of 2nd smoke helmet per man & use of respirator to be discontinued - 2 helmets to be carried by each man and one held in battalion reserve.	15 May
	8	-	4th Corps No 2625 3/8 re issue of special smoke helmets for machine gunners only. Pending large output from factory.	15 May
	9	-	Steps to be completed with smoke helmet from the Reserve the Reserve completed by demand - authority 4th Corps 2625 (Q) O.S/14/72.	15 May
	10	-	O.S. 48/144. 9/8/15. Proviso smoke helmets to have 10% of the strength with division.	15 May
	12	-	Steno sights allotted to division G. et C.L.	15 May

WAR DIARY or INTELLIGENCE SUMMARY

Army Form C. 2118

DADOS XV Dvn
August 15

Folio 2.

Place	Date August	Hour	Summary of Events and Information	Remarks and references to Appendices
Continued :-	14	-	4"Corps 2625 O.C./48/90 11/8/15:- Demands to be put forward for Goggles for artillery gunners at the rate of 2 per battery. (Goggles antigaz, rubber, film exposure)	To Maj. To Maj.
	15	-	O.S/48/90/12 14/8/15:- Respirators Non mnnmnmn replaced by 2nd smoke helmets to be retained.	To Maj.
	15	-	54/Arty/6451 5/8/15 G.H.Q. Q/36/5. Increase Veterinary establishment of N.CO. R.F.A. brigades.	To Maj.
	16	-	O.S/35/16 13/8/15. Allotment of 1 telescope gunners & antiaircraft section XV division.	To Maj.
	17	-	O.S.P/1485/ O.S. 11/87 16/8/15... Special tools for brigade armament artificers to carry out repairs to No 7 dial sights.	To Maj.
	17	-	Notification received from HAVRE that light bipod mountings to Lewis machine guns are not allowed in addition to the usual IV mountings.	To Maj.
	18	-	O.S/7/49 16/8/15 Decided to fix scale of periscopes at 8/per battalion.	To Maj.
	18	-	Allotment of N6 acid and fire proof suits to issue to the division 08/163/1. 10/8/15.	To Maj.
	18	-	Two rifles with telescopic sights allotted by 4" Corps to XV Div.	To Maj.
	18	-	Two "White division optical sights" allotted by 4" Corps to XV Division	To Maj.
	22	-	O.S/6/17 20/8/15 .. 4"Corps 5021 .. 21/8/15 :-. Withdrawal of pistols from 3 Surplus per battalion.	To Maj.
	23	-	O.S.47/18 21/8/15 :- Issue of 1 harp-shaped periscope to all artillery brigades to time..	To Maj.
	25	-	O.S.B/129 20/8/15 Indents for machine guns required to replace lost or unserviceable not to be mnnnnmm repeated to D.O.S. in future.	To Maj.

WAR DIARY or INTELLIGENCE SUMMARY

Army Form C. 2118

DADOS XV Div
August 1915
Folio 3

Place	Date August	Hour	Summary of Events and Information	Remarks and references to Appendices
Concluded	26	-	O.S/8/87..26/8/15..4th Corps 5106...Hyperscopes unavailable for Lewis guns - indents not to be submitted.	15th May
	27	-	O.S.R/1826..O.S/12/15..25/8/15..Local purchase, Officers from English firms, form of prop to	30 May
	27	-	O.S/13/108..25/8/15..Repairs to vehicles and replacements of pole props, tailboards? etc: to be carried out locally.	30 May
Head Qrs XV Div	30	-	O.S.R/1973..O.S/17/15..29.8.15..Local purchase of up £100 of any one description of Store - authority of D.O.S. to be first obtained.	1st May
	30	-	G.H.Q/264..O.S/26/10..29.8.15..Blankets at the rate of one per man..to be indented for.	15th May

J Smith Major
DADOS XV D.
2/9/15

Confidential

WAR DIARY

OF

D.A.D.O.S. – XV. DIVISION

From 1st September to 30th September 1915

(Major F. Smith
A.O.D.)

DADOS XV Div'n — WAR DIARY or INTELLIGENCE SUMMARY — September 1915 — Army Form C. 2118

Instructions regarding War Diaries and Intelligence Summaries are contained in F. S. Regs., Part II. and the Staff Manual respectively. Title Pages will be prepared in manuscript.

(Erase heading not required.)

Place	Date	Hour	Summary of Events and Information	Remarks and references to Appendices
Headquarters XV. Division.	September			
	3		O.S. 63/1 31/8/15 4° Corps 44494 (Q) — Number of Acid and fireproof suits for issue to 15 division now fixed at 166.	20/
	5		O.S. 7/70 3/9/15 Rifles for grenade firing — 16 per battalion allowed.	21/
	6		O.S.A./5010 3/9/15. O.S. 21/43 5/9/15 — Indents to be checked by D.O.O³	22/
	9		O.S./121B. 9.9.15. Application for approval for all purchases over £25 to be sent through Divisional and Corps Commanders.	23/
	9		O.S. 48/210. 9.9.15. Instructions re moves of units reporting to BASE and ABBEVILLE.	24/
	10		O.S./14/104. 9.9.15. Grenade badges authorized for infantry and pioneer battalions	25/
	10		Offrs. 9.9.15	
	11		Carriage Q.F. 18 pr. Complete with sights, one, C Battery 71st Bde. crews' fire and replaced.	26/
	13		O.S. 31/51 12.9.15. Issue of Soyers stoves 50 per division authorized	27/
	13		Ordnance Q.F. 4.5 inch howitzer complete with carriage and dial sight — 1 C battery 73rd totally unserviceable by gun-burst, replaced	28/

WAR DIARY or INTELLIGENCE SUMMARY

D.A.D.O.S. XV. Corps September '15 Army Form C. 2118

Place	Date	Hour	Summary of Events and Information	Remarks and references to Appendices
Headquarters XV Corps	Sept 17	—	Railhead CHOCQUES	72
	19	—	O.S. 13/117 (Q 3470) 18/9/15. Authorizes Special transport scale for Special Companies R.E.	73
	21	—	O.S. 54/30 20/9/15. All purchases of handcarts over £25 should be reported to D.D.O.S. Army for covering approval.	74
	22	—	O.S. 48/10 21/9/15. Anti-gas goggles to be revised at the increased rate of 1 per officer and man.	75
	22	—	O.S. 48/273 20/9/15. Cases where boots lasting refills are an A.O.D. Supply.	76
	22	—	O.S. 21/46 21.9.15. Queries from HAVRE to be referred to D.D.O.S. 1st Army by D.A.D.O.S. in certain cases.	77
	23	—	O.S. 27/27. 22.9.15. No more sandbags to be purchased locally, without order of D. of O.S.	78
	23	—	O.S./8/55 22/9/15. Faults in feed blocks Vickers machine guns, being of 1st Army to be sent up	79
	23	—	O.S. 22/19 22/9/15. Bicycles – including of in list of stores in bulk.	80
	23	—	O.S./53/3 22.9.15 List of component parts of Catapults West Bomb throwers	81

DADOS XV Divn   WAR DIARY   September   Army Form C. 2118
                 or
                 INTELLIGENCE SUMMARY
                 Concluded
                 (Erase heading not required.)

Place	Date	Hour	Summary of Events and Information	Remarks and references to Appendices
Headquarters XV Divn	Sept. 23	—	O.S. 48/221. 20.9.15. Question of cancelling outstanding indents and redemanding	
	24	—	O.S./32/219. 23.9.15. Issue of store to Army postal services authority in appendix IV of manual.	
	24	—	Received 500 magazines for Lewis machine guns from HAVRE	
	25	—	" 600 " " CALAIS	
	25	—	" 550 " " HAVRE	
	25	—	Telegram Ot. 1st Army O.S/5231. 25/9/15. Asking for approximate total ration going to be complete Division 61 officers and men.	
	27	—	Railhead NOEUX LES MINES.	
	27	—	O.S 54/30 25/9/15. Handcarts to travel with batteries - to be procured ander Foy officer in Conjunction with T.Q.M.	

Signature
DADOS XV Dn
2/10/15

121/7431

15th Division

A.Q. 15th Div: 87802.
Vol: 4
Oct 15

WAR DIARY

D.A.D.O.S. XV DIVISION

October 1915

Duplicate War Diary
dated July 15
enclosed

Sent separately T320.
To Mmaster
[signature]
9/4/15

SECRET

WAR DIARY of INTELLIGENCE SUMMARY

DADOS XV Div — October 1915 — Army Form C. 2118.

Place	Date	Hour	Summary of Events and Information	Remarks and references to Appendices
October	1st		Ordnance depôt moved from HESDIGNEUL to LA BUISSIÈRE. Railhead LILLERS	App
	3rd		" " LA BUISSIÈRE to LAPUGNOY	App App App
	10th		O.S. 8/111. 7.10.15. Method of carrying the Lewis Machine gun will web rifle sling	
	10th		O.S. 43/36 7.10.15. Bags intrenching tools being sent out for Pioneer battalion	App
	10th		O.S. 7/98 7.10.15. Exchange of long rifles sighted for Mk VII ammunition - unsecured and	
	10th		O.S. 48/141 6.10.15. How Brazier allowed for the division	App App
	15		Ordnance depôt moved from LAPUGNOY to NOEUX LES MINES	
	16		O.S. 20/12 14.10.15. Issue of frost nails. Frost cogs not available until 1st Nov.	
	16		Railhead NOEUX LES MINES	App App App
	17		O.S. 62/1 15.10.15 Issue of field forges to Heavy Batteries and Div'l Amm' Column	App App App
	17		O.S. 7/90 16.10.15 Withdrawal of Rhino from all Stretcher bearers	
	19		O.S. 15/14. 17.10.15 Bottles tin oil no longer to be issued	
	21		O.S. 1/76 20.10.15 Issue of 4000 pairs gum boots for use of men in the trenches	App App App
	21		O.I. 64/1 11.10.15 Introduction of the steel helmet - 50 per battalion	
	23		O.I. 48/90/12 19.10.15 "Drill pattern" tube helmets, 400 for the division	App App App
	23		O.I. 27/22 20.10.15 Traversor made not required - to be returned to its base	

D.A.D.O.S. 15th D.   October Continued   Army Form C. 2118.

WAR DIARY
INTELLIGENCE SUMMARY
(Erase heading not required.)

Place	Date	Hour	Summary of Events and Information	Remarks and references to Appendices
	25	—	O.O./54/30 24.10.15. Handcarts for trench mortar batteries	709
	27	—	O.O./14/117 26.10.15. Undercoats fur — to be issued to Infantry units at the front.	709
	29	—	O.O./62/1 28.10.15 Field forge substituting Anvil petrol flare lamp.	709

James Major
D.A.D.O.S. 15 D.

Hq. 15th Division
S.A.A.G.
Vol. 5

121/76/8

Nov 15

WAR DIARY

D.A.D.O.S. XV DIVISION

NOVEMBER 1915

WAR DIARY
INTELLIGENCE SUMMARY

DADOS 15 Div
Army Form C. 2118.

November 1915

Place	Date	Hour	Summary of Events and Information	Remarks and references to Appendices
November				
	3		O/48/90/2. 31/10/15. Pockets to ensure helmets in future to be dismounted of as reg.	707
	4		OG/83/44/402 28/10/15. Proposition to be issued in preference to the hypo pattern but are to be replaced by like pattern helmets immediately available	707
	5		1st Army N° 2735 Q. 4.11.15. Expenditure of 50 francs per brigade area to furnish furniture to each Rec Room actually established	707
	6		OA/24/22. 1.11.15. Cartridge electric signalling lamps allotted to the dist of troops	707
	6		OA/31/38 5.11.15. Lanterns tent folding 400 per division authorized	707
	6		OA R/2521. 3.11.15 weekly return of local purchases exceeding £25 introduction of Army Form W 3336	707
	8		OA/8/118 3.11.15. Proper machine gun shield 1 allotted to the div for trial	707
	8		OA/14/11 7.11.15. Balmoral Bonnets. Small reserve of to be maintained	707
	14		OA/8/91 13.11.15 Experimental handcart for Lewis guns. Stores supplied Div transport	707
	14		OA/8/113 12.11.15 Cups muzzle for Hotckiss gun local pattern to be replaced by service patt.	707
	14		OA/8/119. 12.11.15. Special Khaki paint for casing of Lewis gun introduction	707
	14		OA/7/109 13.11.15 Reg C. of bottles for the personnel of machine gun batteries to battery equip?	707
	15		OA/38/147 10.11.15 Alteration in the designation of Inspector of ordnance Machinery	707

WAR DIARY

DADoS 15 'Div' November Continued

Army Form C. 2118

INTELLIGENCE SUMMARY

(Erase heading not required.)

Place	Date	Hour	Summary of Events and Information	Remarks and references to Appendices
	November			
	15		OO/30/40 14.11.15. Wireless receiving sets and elec. signalling lamps for Battalions, Batteries, Bde. H.Qrs. Bdgts and H.Q. division.	760
	15		OO/8/52 13.11.15. Issue of Bipod mountings for Lewis guns restricted issue of the LW.F. tripod	761
	15		OO/18/1501/1745 OO/23/93 12.11.15. Impending introduction of elevating and traversing dials	762
	19		OO/14/146 18/11/15 Restricted issue of Goats' Skin ??? lined and the issue of undercoats fur and leather jerkins	763
	21		OO/14/144 20.11.15. Experimental—Sheath for the aspirad to the shoulder strap to prevent the rifle sling slipping it.	764
	22		OO/9/315 21.11.15. Gunmetal fuze keys to replace locally made pattern	765
	24		OO/11/93 23.11.15 18pr. QF gun carriage to be fitted with a clamp and adjusting arc for clamping the carriage body to the trail	766
	25		OO/13/117 24.11.15. Store for Special Companies RE supply	767

signature

SADD. 16th Div.
Vol: 6

121/7928

D.A.D.O.S.

December 1915.

WAR DIARY or INTELLIGENCE SUMMARY

D.A.D.O.S. XV. Divn.

December 1915

Army Form C. 2118

Place	Date	Hour	Summary of Events and Information	Remarks and references to Appendices
DECEMBER				
	1		Ordnance Depot - NOEUX-LES-MINES. Railhead - NOEUX-LES-MINES.	
	1		O.S/64/1 29/11/15. Issue of steel helmets on scale of one per officer and man of Infantry units.	
	6		O.S/48/50/22 4/12/15. Completion of 2 July pattern smoke helmets for every officer and man, and completion of Div. Resv. 15% scale of per officer & man	
	6		O.S/26/10 5.12.15. Blankets both issued to complete scale of two per man	
	11		O.S/64/1 10.12.15. Steel helmets to be issued to French interpreters attached to units	
	15		Ordnance Depot moved from NOEUX-LES-MINES to AUCHEL. Railhead - LILLERS	
	17		O.S/11/73 15.12.15 Instructions re replacement of Gun trails (i) when unserviceable (ii) when lost – in latter case demands to be again approved of DDOS	
	19		O.S/54/30 18.12.15. Provision of handcarts for T. Mortar Batteries	
	19		O.S/77/113 18.12.15. Issue of tin water bottle stoppers	
	19		O.S/14/166 18.12.15. Approval for maintenance of Div. Resv. of 5000 prs socks	
	19		O.S/48/27 18.12.15. Issue of 6 periscopes to Div. Cavalry	
	20		O.S/43/44 17.12.15 CoO B/2289. H.P.D.G.S. Breechings, small, for use with mules requiring smaller size	

WAR DIARY (concluded)

D.A.D.O.S. XI Div

INTELLIGENCE SUMMARY DECEMBER 1915

Army Form C. 2118

Place	Date	Hour	Summary of Events and Information	Remarks and references to Appendices
Decem[ber]	22		O.S./1/73 22/12/15 Training of men in the repair of gun belts, kits, by skilled workmen	Ap
	23		#A/3	
	24		O.S. 64/ OSA/4930 23.12.15 Notification of introduction of new belt filling machine (scale of 2 per Div.) by Lt. Dransden	Ap
	25		O.S. 27/12 23.12.15 List of Trench Stores	Ap
	26		W.O. Letter 79/8493/A2. 20.12.15 Reinforcement of No 4 Divisional Ar Q. 3/18 p.d.v.	Ap
	27		O.S. 8/93 25.12.15 – Range finder instr. for Machine gun, raised to 2 per Cy.	Ap
	30		Railhead FOUQUEREUIL.	Ap
	31		O.S. 3/39 29.12.15 Alterations re picketing gear for mules	Ap
	31		f. Army 2417/3 Q. Allotment of R.Sy. Horses and Bicycles to Interpreters	Ap

J.S. Hutchins
D.A.D.O.S.
XI Div

D.A.D.O.S. 15th Divn. WAR DIARY — INTELLIGENCE SUMMARY — JANUARY 1915.

Army Form C. 2118.

Place	Date	Hour	Summary of Events and Information	Remarks and references to Appendices
AUCHEL			Railway LILLERS.	
	2		O.S. 24/25 30.12.15. Proposed scheme to minimise wastage in Cllg. "S."	Col
	2		O.S. 14/152 No further issue of shirts in lieu of vests to be made, owing to supplies of white twill.	Col
	5		O.S. 8/9 3. 2/1/16. Haversacks for Lewis guns to be issued later. Demands not to be submitted at present.	Col
	7		O.S. 13/86 5/1/16. Extra G.S. Wagon authorised for conveyance of Divl. Band Instruments. (Auth: O.N. 4. 9/2387 31/1/16)	F—
	7		O.S. 48/90/1 7/1/16. Proposed introduction of new "Spires" Goggles, anti-gas. Maxim Gun Detachments.	Col into flannel lining. Shirts in worsted.
	8		O.S. 7/128 7/1/16. Withdrawal of rifles from Vickers and Maxim Gun Detachments.	Col
	11		O.S. 8/107 9/1/16. Disappearing mountings detailed in G.R.O. 1030 cancelled for Lewis Guns.	Col
	12		O.S. 48/409 10/1/16. Q.M.G. 3629. 9/1/16 — Substitution of bicycles for similar no. of horses for R.A.	Col.
	15		O.S. 48/276 13/1/16. O.O.S. 115/12/A. Provision being made for issue of wire cutters for fixing to rifles on scale of 64 per Batt. + Corps reserve of 2000.	Col
			Ordnance Depot — NOEUX-LES-MINES. and Raillots.	
	15		O.S. 48/453 13/1/16. Local allotment of interior fittings for Fords W/w Ambulances to F.A.W. Units.	Col
	15		O.S. 64/1 13/1/16. Cancellation of issue of steel helmets to small Infantry attached.	Col
	15		O.S. 48/70 13/1/16. Authorisation of 100 more veils for division, making issue now 350.	Col
	17		O.S. 42/17/1. 16/1/16. Elwood knapshapts Persepose allotted to Divn as an alternative to No. 14 pending issue of latter.	Col

Army Form C. 2118

WAR DIARY
or
INTELLIGENCE SUMMARY

D.A.D.O.S. 15 Div.   January 1916 (continued)

Place	Date	Hour	Summary of Events and Information	Remarks and references to Appendices
NOEUX LES MINES	20		D.G. 280/2/38 d/13/1/16	8
	21		1324/38 A.Q. O.S. 48/90/29 Introduction of special Kuhl helmet with rubber sponge rims to Artillery in scale of 24 per Battery	8
			O.S. 48/409. 21/1/16. Two bicycles in lieu of horses to be indented for and issued to Battmn. of Artillery	8
	22		O.S. 30/55. 21.1.16. Issue of Pattern netchair 9" x Drills, etc to Div. Signal Cy. D.O.S. O.S. A/5304/16	8
	24		O.S. 48/75/1. 22.1.16. Issue of Vermorel Sprayers increased to 100 per Infantry Division	8
	25		O.S. 48/90/32. 24.1.16. 5000 'P' Tube Helmets demanded from Base for Div. Reserve @ O.S. 317/3/A	8
	26		O.S. 9/348. 20.1.16. 2250 rounds Armour piercing S.A.A. ·303" allotted to 15 Div. for trial.	8
	30		O.S. 54/11 26.1.16. No 4 pdr. Mortars or personnel available for issue for replacements but states to be submitted to Ordnance Officers concerned.	8

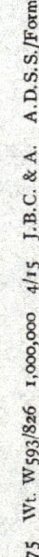

d. A. D. C. 15.ᵗᵉ Div:
vol: 8

WAR DIARY or INTELLIGENCE SUMMARY

Army Form C. 2118

DADOS. 15 Div.

FEBRUARY 1916

Place	Date	Hour	Summary of Events and Information	Remarks and references to Appendices
NOEUX-LES-MINES	Feby. 1		0/14721 Pte Chaotey, A.O.C., gave instruction to units of this Division in repair of gum boots. (Transferred to 47 Div 14.2.16)	Sgd
	1		(OS 54/45/1 d/29.1.16) Lt Syers, M.G.C.'s being allotted to 15 Div. only 8 sent to Lt Corps	Sgd
	3	1400	P.H. Smoke Helmets received for issue as protection for war — this being emergency issue	
	5	300	Acid proof suits received for issue to machine gunners in front line trenches. Ack Q.O.S. 317/29/A	Sgd
	9	2532	"C" Battery 70 B'de. have an 18 pdr QF gun put out of action by enemys fire — verified by I.O.M. Lims Base for replacement.	Sgd Sgd
	10		Steel Trench Helmets demand for Base. Ack. 08/64/1. 8.2.16	Sgd Sgd
	10	7	Skilos MgNars, No4, being allotted to 15 Div (Lt Corps Q/727.7.2.16. To be gvm to B/45(3) + D/46(4)	Sgd
	12		"C" Battery 72 B'de had an 18 pdr QF gun put out of action through burst – verified by I.O.M. lims Base for replacement.	Sgd Sgd
	12		Divl Branch Machine Gun Companies armn.	Sgd Sgd
	13		1 No 23 Respirator for war with Binoculars received – issued to H.Q. 46 Inf Bde	Sgd Sgd
	14		DADOS. 1st Army visit this Depot.	Sgd Sgd
	21	4500	P.H. Helmets issued for (to complete Division) scale of one per officer and man. (Auth: OS W2 8006 21.2.16)	Sgd Sgd
	24		OS.24/51. 22.2.16. Q.O.S. 142/5/A Periscopes issued to Heliographers.	Sgd Sgd
	26		OS.9/1/1. 23.2.16. 4 Maxim guns in charge of Lt Suffolks both replaced by Lewis Guns.	Sgd Sgd
	27		1/4 Suffolks leave Division to join 33rd Division	Sgd Sgd

Dados
is 423
Vol 9

D.A.D.O.S. XV Div.

WAR DIARY
or
INTELLIGENCE SUMMARY

Army Form C. 2118

MARCH 1916

Place	Date	Hour	Summary of Events and Information	Remarks and references to Appendices
NOEUX-LES-MINES	2		Reconstitution of 4th & 1st Corps — 15th Div. to be included in 1st Corps from 10 a.m. 2/3/16. IV Corps O.O. 702 d/1/3/16	Sd
	2		O.S. 48/90/2 29.2.16. Issue of 2 scenes satchel for carrying anti-gas helmet apparatus.	Sd
	11		4 Mortars (3.7") recvd from I.O.M. S. Section — issued to 44th Bde.	Sd
	11		3 Lewis Snipersopes received from 1st Army R.A. Workshops issued to 11th M.M. Gun Battery for Divl. School	Sd
	12		1 — 2" Mortar from Mortar School, ST-VENANT, issued to 63 T.M. Battery	Sd
	12		126 Box Respirators recvd from 16th Div — issued 56 each to 44th & 46th Brigades, & 20 to D.A.	Sd
			1730 of new Respirators are in store being allotted to Div. for use of Machine Gunners and Artillery Gunners under O.S. 48/90/35 dated 26/2/16	Sd
	13		C.O.O. B/1877. 11.3.16. Protractors issued G.R.O. 1371 to be withdrawn & new & older pattern (non-Gallicilly) issued	Sd
	13		Alteration of nomenclature of Trench Mortar Batteries — O.S. 54/45 a/3/3/16.	Sd
	15		Notified under O.S. 48/468/3 13/3/16 that 1st Corps will be based on CALAIS for Ordnance Stores. Lorry issues in present bases should reach HAVRE on 24th instant	Sd
	16		3 Stombos Horns recvd for experimental purposes. Issued to H.Q. of the Brigades inline and D.A.H.	Sd
	17		19000 P.H. Smith helmets issued for use next times from 1st Corps to complete scale of the per other and men	Sd
	12		19040 P.H. Helmets received	Sd
	20		7340 Pte Crowder, Reinf. — A.O.C. sent as reinforcement from Base to complete establishment.	Sd
			O/2461 Sgt. Norman E. sent up for duty with A.D.O.S. 1st Corps. 18/3/16	Sd
	24		4 Rifle Batteries recvd for trial. To be tried and to return Divisional	Sd
	27		Ordnance Depot moved to LILLERS	Sd

Geoffrey H. H. Milne
DADOS 15 Dist.

D.A.D.O.S. 15th Div. WAR DIARY — INTELLIGENCE SUMMARY

April 1916

Place	Date	Hour	Summary of Events and Information	Remarks and references to Appendices
LILLERS	2		O.S.11/199/2 dated 1/4/16. No 7 Dial Sights to be now demanded to replace No 1 Dial Sights in possession of 18 pdr. Batteries of the 15th Div. on scale of 1 per gun. Amm¹ Column to retain one No 1 Dial Sight as spare.	Sv
	2		O.S. 48/409 dated 26/3/16. Bicycles (2) in lieu of horses to be extended to H.Q.R.A., and H.Q. R.F.A. Bdes. Saddlery to be withdrawn on receipt of bicycles and sent to Base.	Sv
	10		4 S/G&o 3" Mortars received from O.O. 1st Corps Dumps. Issued 1 to 44th, 1 to 45th, as 2 to 46 Inf/ 130th be 2" Trench Mortars received from 16th Division. Issued to T/15 T.M. Battery 11/4/16.	Sv
	11		18000 P.H. Helmets demanded from Base to complete Divisional Reserve (O.S. 48/90/31 d/9/4/16)	Sv
	13		4000 P.H. Helmets to be retained (from those withdrawn from troops to receive issue of 2" P.H.) for Drill purposes. (Auth. G.H.Q. O/B/215 5.4.16).	Sv
	13ᵃ		Notification that 5000 covers for steel helmets will be issued to Div from Calais through 1st Corps. O.S.64/1/2. 10.4.16	Sv
	15		18000 P.H. Helmets received for Divl Reserve.	Sv
	15		O.S 48/90/45. 13/4/16 — 1800 Box Respirators and 1900 P.H.G. Helmets indented for in bulk according to scale given in this letter.	Sv
	18		Statement sent to A.A. and Q.M.G. 15th Div. re long issues of S.D. Clothing in this Division during past three weeks.	hy.

Army Form C. 2118.

D.A.D.O.S 15 Div.

WAR DIARY or INTELLIGENCE SUMMARY.

April 1916 continued

(Erase heading not required.)

Instructions regarding War Diaries and Intelligence Summaries are contained in F. S. Regs., Part II. and the Staff Manual respectively. Title pages will be prepared in manuscript.

Place	Date	Hour	Summary of Events and Information	Remarks and references to Appendices
LILLERS	21		500 Steel Helmets received from 16th Division.	Sd.
	21		O.S. 54/16/2. 19/4/16 Indents for 2" Trench Mortars to be sent in future to HAVRE.	Sd.
	23		800 Covers for Steel Helmets received from O.O.I. Corps Troops	Sd.
			4 2" Stokes Mortars received from ST VENANT and handed to X/15 Medium T.M. Battery, Yu	Sd.
			1.5" Mortars returned to HAVRE 23/4/16 O.S. 54/16/2 dated 19.4.16.	Sd.
	27		Ordnance Depot moved to BETHUNE.	Sd.
	27		700 P.H. Helmets drawn from Corps Store to replace unserviceable after gas attack 27/4/16	Sd.
BETHUNE	28		Railhead BETHUNE.	Sd.
	30		Divisional Ammunition Shop started - with 7 Armourers.	Sd.

[signature]
D.A.D.O.S
15th Div.

WAR DIARY
INTELLIGENCE SUMMARY

D.A.D.O.S.
15th DIVISION
Vol II

Army Form C. 2118.

MAY 1916

Place	Date	Hour	Summary of Events and Information	Remarks and references to Appendices
BETHUNE	1		Divisional Boot Shop opened for repairing boots of units not provided with Shoemakers	
	7		8th Gordon Hldrs. and 6th Royal Scots Fusiliers joined 15 Division from 9th Division	
	12	10.5.16	XI Corps O.S. 12/4 B Squadron 1/1 Lothians and Cumberland Yeomanry leave Division to amalgamate and form part of XI Corps Cavalry Regiment.	
	12	10.5.16	O.S. 64/1/3 Steel Helmets to personnel of First Army to be issued with special light abdominal pads. This not to commit us re Calais.	
	12		O.S. 1/7. 9/5/16. Notification of forthcoming Army Order authorising issue of Shoemakers tools H33 on scale of 2 per Inf. Battalion and 1 per Batting R.A. To be treated as items under G.R.O.	
	14		10th Highland Light Infantry and 11th Highland Light Infantry joined 15 Division form 9th Division - prior to 46th Infantry Brigade.	
			8th Gordon Highlanders and 10th Gordon Highlanders amalgamated to form "8/10th Gordon Hldrs."	
	19	O.S. 64/1/3 17/5/16	Painting of Steel Helmets with light drab paint - to be done locally or at No. 24 Ordnance Workshops under Corps arrangements.	
	20		6th and 7th Battns. R.S. Fusiliers amalgamated to form 6/7 R.S. Fusiliers	
	21		5 Stokes 3" Mortars received from O.O. I Corps. Troops issued 4 to 44th, 1 to 46, 13th Bdes	
	22		Fullest issue of 2 Bicycles in place of Horses approved to all Bde. H.Q. R.F.A. Batteries and H.Q. D.A. under O.S. 48/409 19.5.16	

WAR DIARY
or
INTELLIGENCE SUMMARY

Army Form C. 2118

Month: May
DADOS 15 Div

Place	Date	Hour	Summary of Events and Information	Remarks and references to Appendices
BETHUNE	22		Issue of Broder pattern, knitted pattern and bell bag pattern french carriers approved under O.S. 9/113 app A 19/5/16 in reference to G.R.O. 1572	A/E
	22		O.S. 2526/888/4 17/5/16 decides that unserviceable uniforms and clothing can now be sent to Base for transmission to England	E
	22		Q.O.S. 9/1148/A authorises issue of Infant's Equipment to R.A. personnel of Motor T.A. Battery	E
	23		Notification that Calais will shortly cease Base for all returns of stores except complete kinds. D.O.S. O.S R3/2549 17.5.16	E
	24		2" Trench Mortars, 18 pdr. Q.F. 4.5" Howitzers, ammunition supplies from Calais. O.S. 13. 1/2549 21/5/16	E
	29		Amalgamation of 7 and 8 Batt. K.O.S. Borderers into 7/8 K.O.S. B.	E
	31		4 kinifgun wheeers fm 7 KOSB's is surplus and returns to Base	E

Harrison & Sons, Printers, St. Martin's Lane, W.C.
(M 4220) Wt. w. 13345—4182. 2500m 2/16   Forms C. 348/61

Army Form C. 348.

MEMORANDUM.

From

To

D.A.G. 3º Echelon
Base

_____1st July_____ 1916.

Herewith War Diary
for June 1916
forwarded under
instructions G.R.O.
1548.

[signature]
DADOS
15 Div

From

To

ANSWER.

_____ 191 .

[Stamp: 1/7/16 15th DIVISION]

Army Form C. 2118.

WAR DIARY
for
INTELLIGENCE SUMMARY.
(Erase heading not required.)

Vol. 12

JUNE 1916.

D.A.D.O.S. 15th Division.

Instructions regarding War Diaries and Intelligence Summaries are contained in F.S. Regs., Part II. and the Staff Manual respectively. Title pages will be prepared in manuscript.

Place	Date	Hour	Summary of Events and Information	Remarks and references to Appendices
BETHUNE	5		GHQ. O.S. 317/5/2/A 31/5/16. Extension of issue of Box respirators and *"P.H."* Helmets to one per unit Gunners. 4 – 3" Stokes Mortars received from I Corps. Issued 1 to 44" Bde. 3 to 45" Bde.	Sd/
	9		O.S. 38/5. 7.6.16. Return Indents for replacement of Guns and Instruments & spare rifles no. 1 piece cartridges.	Sd/
	10		O.S. 8/16/2. 8.6.16. Ammunition returns to G.R.O. 1616 to be withdrawn from Batts: for return to Base	Sd/
	13		O.S. 64/1. 10/6/16. Extension of issue of Steel Helmets with regard to O.S. 64/1. 8/1/16	Sd/
	14		First Army circular No. 347/1. Q. 11.6.16 re allocation & establishing of rifles in D.A. Column.	Sd
	16		O.S. 54/45. 14.6.16. The Six light Trench Mortar Batty's. of each of 1st Div to be Grouped together into one Battery of the Section of 4 Mortars each.	Sd
	17		9 Howitzer Stokes Mortars received. Issued 2 to 44", and 7 to 45" Trench Mortar Batteries, completing Division up to 8 per T.M. Battery.	Sd
	17		One motor cycle raising and sent to Ordnance Workshop (Light) to be held for new 15 Division under D.O.S. O.S.D. 1/2557 7/6/16.	Sd
	21 19 16		15 Div. Cyclist Coy. left Division to join I Corps Cyclist Battalion.	Sd
	23		2 – 4in. Stokes Mortars received from O.O. I Corps Dumps.	Sd
	25		Railway – NOEUX-LES-MINES.	
	27		Wind for 26 lews Guns from HAVRE to complete Division to 6 per Battalion under authority D.O.S. O.S.D. 1/1315/2 – 27/6/16.	Sd
	30		180" Tunnelling Coy R.E. and 15 Divnl. Sub-Park come under 15 Div for Ordnance Services	Sd

Sd/ J. B. Humphrey
D.A.D.O.S. 15th Div.

WAR DIARY.
JULY 1916

Army Ordnance Department.
D.A.D.O.S. 15th Division

WAR DIARY

D.A.D.O.S. 15 Div. Army Form C. 2118

INTELLIGENCE SUMMARY

JULY 1916

(Erase heading not required.)

Place	Date	Hour	Summary of Events and Information	Remarks and references to Appendices
BETHUNE	1		253rd Tunnelling Coy. under Division for Ordnance Services.	—
	2		197 Land Drainage Coy under Division for Ordnance Services	—
"	2		26 Lewis machine guns received from Base. This completes Division to scale of 6 per Inf. Batt.	—
	7		One P.H.G Helmet per officer & man authorized, except in case of men whose pattern with Box Respirators. O&Q 30/15/1959 7.7.16	—
	11		2 Bicycles in keeping stores authorised for HQ D.A., Bde. HQ, R.A. & each Battery R.F.A. Instruc'ns 48/409 9/7/16	—
	12		1 45 Howitzer received from Base for B/70. To replace N.477 burst.	—
	23		Ordnance Depot moved to GROSSART, nr BRYAS (ST POL). Railhead LILLERS.	—
	26		Moved to FLERS	—
	27		Moved to FROHEN-LE-GRAND	—
	28		Ordnance Depot — BERNAVILLE. Railhead ROQUEMAISON. Under X Corps for administration.	—
	29		Railhead VIGNACOURT. Based on HAVRE from 28/7/16.	—
			Two extra Lewis Guns per Battalion making complement of 8 per Batt., authorized for by authority D.D.O.S. Reserve Army R/87 27/7/16. Died for.	—
	31		Moved to VIGNACOURT. C/70 Bty has 3 Q.F. 18 pdr. guns condemned by 1 O.M Reserve Army. Replacement urgently	—

1/8/1916.

Jeffrey H.M. Capt.
DADOS
15 Division

Original

WAR DIARY

D.A.D.O.S. 15th Division

Period. 1st – 31st August 1916

D.A.D.o.S.
WAR DIARY
15th DIVISION INTELLIGENCE SUMMARY. AUGUST 1916

Army Form C. 2118.

Place	Date	Hour	Summary of Events and Information	Remarks and references to Appendices
VIGNACOURT	1		Railhead HANGEST S/ SOMME. Division complete up to 8 Lewis Guns per Battalion	
	4		Moved to ST. GRATIEN	
	5		Moved to BAIZIEUX. – 72 Halberts rec'd from Base (for Lewis Guns). Issued 6 to each Inf: Batt:	
	8		Ordnance Depot – ALBERT-AMIENS Road E/8/a – 470 had one 18 pdr gun and carriage damaged by hostile fire. Replacement wired for.	
	14		0/17774 Pte WATKISS B. arrived as reinforcement	
	15		B/72 had one 18 pdr gun damaged by hostile fire. Replacement wired for. Great difficulties in obtaining Steel Helmets. Base state no men will be forthcoming for some time. All reinforcements arrive without same. Salvage company not enabled to cope with supplies, which can only be got with difficulty from Railhead.	
			4571 Pte WHEELER. A.O.C. left to join O.O. III Corps Troops for duty as clerk. 9/3454 Pte C. LUSCOMBE arrived for duty from O.O. III Corps Divisn as replacement.	
ALBERT	17		A/73 have one @ 3.18 pdr gun extrance for new and serving Replacement wired for.	
	23			
	26		Many units ie 7 103rd Inf: Bde., (34th Div.), join 15th Div. as an attached for Ordnance Service from 21/8/16. HQ 103rd Inf: Bde. 24, 25, 26 and 27 Batt: Northumberland Fusiliers, 18 Batt: (Pioneer) Northumberland Fusiliers, 103rd Machine Gun Co, 103rd Trench Mortar Bty, N4 Co, 34th Divl: Train.	

WAR DIARY
or
INTELLIGENCE SUMMARY

Army Form C. 2118.

AUGUST 1916

D.A.D.O.S
15th Div.

Place	Date	Hour	Summary of Events and Information	Remarks and references to Appendices
ALBERT	26		15th Amm Sub Park transferred to III Corps Troops for Ordnance Services	
	27		5559 a/Sub. C Strutt COCKRAM, S. O/5245 Pte PACK H.G. and O/8709 Pte ORR, S/AOC attached (for 103rd Bde Group)	
	28		13/73 13th have 2 18pr guns and carriages and 13/72 13th 1 18pr gun and carriage condemned to I.O.M. through damage by hostile fire. Replacements insist for.	
	30		2000 Small Arms Ammo received from Base.	
	31		Return of Machine Guns and Mortars for which replacements have been indented for during period 1/8/16 to 31/8/16	

Machine Guns: Lewis

9" Black Watch	- 3	13 R Scots nil
8/10 Gordon Hldrs	- 3	6/7 R Scots Fusil. 1
7 Cameron	- 3	8 Seaforth nil
8 Seaforth Hldrs	- nil	11" Argyll & Suth Hldrs - 1
	9	2

7/8 KOSB — 1
15th Scot: Rifles nil
10/11 H.L.I. — 2
12 H.L.I. — 1
Total 4

Total 15.

Machine Guns Vickers

44 M. Gun Coy. 3   45 M. Gun Coy nil   46 M. Gun Coy 2
Total 5

Mortars: Stokes

44 T M Btty 1   45 T M Btty 2   46 T M Btty nil
Total 3.

Jeffy Wathon
DADOS 15 Div

Vol 15

WAR DIARY
SEPTEMBER, 1916

D.A.D.O.S.
15th Divn.

Thos. De La Rue & Co. Ltd., Bunhill Row, E.C.
W3125/1706 1,200m 6/15

Forms
C. 348
61

Army Form C. 348.

No._____

MEMORANDUM.

From

To

From

To

ANSWER.

_____

_____191

_____

_____191

Army Form C. 2118.

WAR DIARY

D.A.D.O.S. 15th Divn. INTELLIGENCE SUMMARY.

SEPTEMBER 1916

(Erase heading not required.)

Instructions regarding 'War Diaries and Intelligence Summaries are contained in F. S. Regs., Part II. and the Staff Manual respectively. Title pages will be prepared in manuscript.

Place	Date	Hour	Summary of Events and Information	Remarks and references to Appendices
ALBERT	2		B Battery 72: Bde. have one 18 pdr. gun and 2 carriages condemned & destroyed & Vehicles fin. Replacements indented for.	
	2		All remaining Spring Q.S. 18pdr. Vehs. to be handed in to Corps Workshops on receipt from Ypdownic Rifles Repairing Repair to be sent to South Army Telescopic Rifle Shop, ANT. NOYELLES	
	2		A Battery 71 Bde. have one old 18 pdr gun destroyed, and one carriage condemned & I.O.M. Replacements indented for.	
	4		Ordnance Depot. moved 800 yards further back up Amiens road on account of shells fire.	
	7		B Battery 70 Bde. have one 18 pdr. and carriage unfit and unserviceable to provisional on been Replacement indented for.	
	17		B/71 have one 4.5 How. and carriage condemned for formation is been Replaced unfit. C/73 have one 18 pdr. gun condemned for use. Replacement indented for.	
	20		Ordnance Depot moved to MONTIGNY	
MONTIGNY	21		Railhead FRECHENCOURT.	
	23		A Battery 72 Bde have one 18 pdr gun condemned & sorry. Replacement unfit for Supplies for Bear on the whole was good during period of re-equipping (i.e. from 20 - 30 Sept.) - also supply of motorism for parts must improve	

J. Hutchinson
D.A.D.O.S. 15 D.N.

War Diary.
October. 1916.

D.A.D.O.S. 15th Div.

Army Form C. 2118.

VOL 16

WAR DIARY

INTELLIGENCE SUMMARY.

D.A.D.O.S. 15 DIV.

OCTOBER 1916

(Erase heading not required.)

Place	Date	Hour	Summary of Events and Information	Remarks and references to Appendices
MONTIGNY.	1		Issues of Winter Clothing – G.R.O. 1824 – commences	A
ALBERT-AMIENS ROAD	13		Ordnance Depot moved to D.12.d.9.0. on 9th October. Railhead ALBERT. Artillery of 23rd Division attached to Ordnance Services. One lorry, one Sergeant, one clerk and one storeman sent as personnel for administration for 23rd Division.	A
	14		A Batty 73rd Bde. han fun N° 594 condemned for sewing in bore. Replacement wired for 31/10/A 7/10/16	A
	15		Div. Reserve of Smoke Helmets (P.H.) to be raised from 2000 to 5000 vide QMG Q.O.S. 7/10/16	A
			Ordnance Depot moved to BECOURT WOOD.	A
BECOURT WOOD	16		D. Battery 72 Bde. han one howitzer and carriage struck by shell fire and damaged. Replacements wired for.	A
	16		A/72 and B/73 han each one 18 pdr gun and carriage condemned for wear, also C/73 one carriage. Replacements for same.	A
	20		A/73 – one gun 18 pdr less B.M. condemned for wear. Replacement for ditto.	A
	22		A/73 han one 18 pdr 1 carriage, A/72 one gun, and B/72 two carriages condemned for sewing and traversing wear. Replacements for same.	A
	24		M/72 han one 18 pdr condemned for sewing in bore – replacement for same	A
	25		C/72 – one carriage 18 pdr condemned	A
	26		A/70 – one Q.F. 18 pdr gun, N° 2561 condemned for sewing in bore } Replacements	A
	27		B/102 – one carriage 18 pdr condemned	A

WAR DIARY
INTELLIGENCE SUMMARY.
(Erase heading not required.)

Army Form C. 2118.

Place	Date	Hour	Summary of Events and Information	Remarks and references to Appendices
RECOURT WOOD	28		R/72 have no carriage endmost. Replacement wand for Second Howitzer authorised by Ordnance.	F
	29		A/104 have 2 – 18 pr. carriages endmost. Replacements awaited	F
			X.Y.Z and V/23 leave 15th Div. to rejoin 23rd Div.	F
			B/102 have 1 OQ.F. 18 pr. carriage endmost. also A/102. Replacements wired for	S/F
			Summary:– Stores have come up remarkably well for Base during the whole of Corps. with the exception of a few technical stores such as siege lamps for Artillery and small items such as bulbs and nipples for electric torches, & first number of these are required under present conditions. There has been no difficulties with regard to supply of guns or carriages.	F

J. H. Wrenbreath
DADOS
1st Div.

Vol #17

WAR DIARY.
NOVEMBER. 1916

D.A.D.O.S. 15th Divn

Officer Commanding.

....

The following is a statement of bulk issues for month of .... to the Unit under your Command.

Nomenclature.	Quantity.	Nomenclature.	Quantity.
Greatcoats		Ropes, head or reims	
Boots, Ankle		Ropes, Heel	
Jackets, S.D.		Ropes, Picketing	
Trousers, S.D.		Mallets, heel peg	
Pantaloons		Sheets, ground	
Caps, S.D.		Oil, lubricating, G.S.	
Puttees		Mineral Jelly	
Shirts		Dubbing	
Drawers, Cotton		Grease, lubricating	
Drawers, Woollen		Soap, yellow	
Socks		Soap, soft	
Vests		Flannelette	
Field Dressings		Pullthroughs—weights	
Smoke Helmets		,, —cords	
Haversacks		,, —gauzes	
Waterbottles		,, —complete	
Mess Tins		Shoes, Horse	
Kettles, Camp		Shoes, Mule	
Bags, Nose		Blankets, G.S.	
Nets, Hay		Tools, Intrenching	
Pegs, Picketing		Cotton Waste	
Posts, Picket		Cloths, Sponge	

Daaremh,
15 Div

Henrik van Dran
for November 1916, phase

Jeffsschuler
Dados 18 Div

30/11 16

WAR DIARY or INTELLIGENCE SUMMARY

Army Form C. 2118.

NOVEMBER 1916
D.A.D.O.S. 15 Division

Place	Date	Hour	Summary of Events and Information	Remarks and references to Appendices
BECOURT WOOD	2		B. Battery 102 Bde. R.F.A. han 18 pdr. gun no. 3375 condemned for scrap.	
	3		Ordnance Depot mard to MILLENCOURT – returned to Ordnance 48' Div.	
MILLENCOURT	4		A Battery 70 Bde R.F.A. han 18 pdr. gun no 5143 condemned for scrap,	
	5		first consignment of "second" blankets arriv.	
	6		Movd to BAIZIEUX. Railed shells ALBERT. Took over for 1st Division.	
BAIZIEUX			Railed trans from FRECHENCOURT on 9th inst.	
	12		Number of guns to be held by Pioneer Battn. sand to 8 O.B. 1362 8/11/16.	
	17		532 Howitzer Battery R.G.A. attached temporarily for Ordnance Service.	
	30		Great difficulties and inconvenience caused by delay in arrival of tracks.	
			despatched from PARIS with blankets and other winter stores.	

Jeffreson Capt
D.A.D.O.S 15. Div.

WAR DIARY Vol 18
DECEMBER 1916

D.A.D.O.S. 15th Div.

Thos. De La Rue & Co. Ltd., Bunhill Row, E.C.
W3125/1706 1,200m 6/15

Forms
C. 348
61

Army Form C. 348.

No._____

MEMORANDUM.

From

From

To

To

ANSWER.

_____

_____

_____191

_____191

Army Form C. 2118

DECEMBER 1916 WAR DIARY or INTELLIGENCE SUMMARY

D.A.D.O.S. 15 D.F.

(Erase heading not required.)

Instructions regarding War Diaries and Intelligence Summaries are contained in F.S. Regs, Part II. and the Staff Manual respectively. Title Pages will be prepared in manuscript.

Place	Date	Hour	Summary of Events and Information	Remarks and references to Appendices
BAIZIEUX	1		Ordnance Depot movd to ALBERT. 69 rue d'AVELUY. Railhead ALBERT.	
ALBERT	3		Reorganisation of 18 pdr. Batteries of 15 DA into 6 gun Batteries. This entails the addition of C/72 and two whls of 73rd Bde. R.F.A.	
	8		Departure of 23rd D.A. to rejoin 23rd Division. (A.D.C. personnel and lorry attached to us leave on same time.) 15.D.A. hands them 3 18 pr. guns to replace deficiencies under III Corps instructions. Notifies that replacements of these are being sent from Third Army.	
	12		Three 18 pdr. guns Nos. 1472. 330 and 580 recvd from Third Army to complete D.A.	
	22		532: Howitzer 1813 (attached) how gun No. 990 + carriage 61983 condemned by Base trench mog., - this howitzer sent back for Special examination	
			Grave difficulties received by troops arriving with out leather jerkins, angora numnah covers without any blankets	
	31		A/70 how gun No. 5340 and carriage 39220 condemned & sent to Base. Grave improvement this month in supplies of gun parts from Base. Stores generally arriving within 2 or 3 days from demand to trucks shortage. A grave deal of paper work for III Corps.	

Jo McCrimmon Capt
D.A.D.O.S. 15 Div

WR19
WAR DIARY
for
JANY 1917.

D.A.D.O.S. 15 Div

Thos. De La Rue & Co. Ltd., Bunhill Row, E.C.
W3125/1706   1,200m   6/15

Forms
C. 348
61

Army Form C. 348.

No._____

MEMORANDUM.

From

From

To

To

ANSWER.

_____   _____191

_____   _____191

D.A.D.O.S 15th DIV. WAR DIARY or INTELLIGENCE SUMMARY JANUARY 1917

Army Form C. 2118

Place	Date	Hour	Summary of Events and Information	Remarks and references to Appendices
ALBERT	1		24 hvis Guns received from Base, completing each Inf. Bde to 12 Guns per Battn.	
	13		Repairs to Guns transferred to Divisional Workshop.	
	14		Notification of impending Artillery reorganisation.	
			Section of C/188 Bde R.F.A. (40th Div) joined 15 Div. and amalgamated with D/71 to form 6 Gun howitzer Battery. (532 Hvy Battrs previously split up between D/70 and D/71 to form 6 Gun howr. Battries.)	
	21		Lieut. B.L. HUMPHRYS A.O.D. joined for duty during temporary absence of Capt. J.G. HARVERT. D.A.D.O.S.	
	24		B/252 (50th [struck: ?] Div) Bde R.F.A. joined D.A. to become C/72. This Battery already possessed 6 18pdr. Guns.	
	25		Smallbox Epidemic - instructions for re-scale of rifles per man.	
	27		Notification of change in organisation of bags & sacks for gas curtains, Bull stores - change to come into force on 29th Jan.	
	28		V/15 T.M. Battery formed with 15th D.A. — at present only equipped with 2 9.45" mortars.	
	31		19000 Shirts, 19000 prs Socks, and 10000 prs Drawers demanded on Base for Div. Laundry exchange during the month & total for the month of 29200 Shirts, 28600 prs socks, and 12000 prs Drawers received for this purpose.	

Vol 20

WAR DIARY.

for FEBRUARY 1917.

D.A.D.O.S. 15th Divn

WAR DIARY

INTELLIGENCE SUMMARY

DADOS 15th Div.

FEBRUARY 1917

Army Form C. 2118.

Place	Date	Hour	Summary of Events and Information	Remarks and references to Appendices
ALBERT	1		72" (Army) Bde. R.F.A. transferred for Ordnance Services to III Corps Troops	
"	3		Moved to BAZIEUX	
BAZIEUX	4		Railhead FRECHENCOURT	
	4		Lieut. HUMPHRYS, D.L. – A.O.D. left me to join DADOS 48' Div for duty	
	7		Whilst with being administered by until futher notice by I. ANZAC Corps from 1/2/17	
	9		24 hour Lewis Guns received for Division. This makes total of 14 per Inf Batt.	
	14		Division move nr. 9 Fuk Army Area. Ordnance with D.H.Q. at BEAUVAL	
BEAUVAL	16		Division was thereafter Ordnance Services – CALMS, & Ordnance Depot - BOQUEMAISON	
BOQUEMAISON	17		Railhead PREVENT. Was administering to VI Corps.	
	18		Moved to ROELLECOURT. - (D.H.Q. at DUISANS).	
ROELLECOURT	19		Railhead ST. POL.	
	25		176m Small Box Respirators received for issue	
	27		3 9.5" Howitzers allotted to Division fm 6 Corps.	

DADOS 15 Div

War Diary.
for March 191(9)
Passed 15.4.19
V.G.T.

Army Form C. 2118.

D.A.D.O.S 15th DIVISION WAR DIARY
INTELLIGENCE SUMMARY
MARCH 1917

Vol 21

Instructions regarding War Diaries and Intelligence Summaries are contained in F.S. Regs., Part II and the Staff Manual respectively. Title pages will be prepared in manuscript.

(Erase heading not required.)

Place	Date	Hour	Summary of Events and Information	Remarks and references to Appendices
ROELLECOURT	1		184. Tunnelling Coy, 5. Entrenching Battn, and N.4 Reserve Gas Coy transferred fm 12. Div. for Ordnance Services. Infantry Battns	
	3		24 mor. Lewis Machine Guns recvd fm Base, completing Division to full scale of 16 per Battn.	
			Lewis helmets withdrawn as failures. - 6 per Inft Batt. - 2 per Pioneers.	
	4		444 Machine Gun Coy transferred to 50. Division for Ordnance Services	
	5		1493. Am. Sub/Pk UNSWORTH. A.O.C. left to join 11. Batt. Leicestershire R.V.	
	8		Mov. to DUISANS. Railhead still ST POL.	
DUISANS	14		½ Coy of 4 Liverpool Regt. (Labour Coy) transferred for Ordnance Services	
	14		Labour Coy (4. Hampshire Regt.) transferred for Ordnance Services	
	18		3 platoons Labour Coy (2. Seaforths) transferred for Ordnance Services	
	17		(Killed) TINCQUES.	
	21		5. Entrenching Battn transferred to O.O. Third Army Troops N.2 for Ordnance Services. Auth: Sixth Corps Ordnance Services W.C. 3319	
	21		444 M.G. Coy returned to Division.	
	23		Division completing up with rubber spray goggles - anti gas	
	27		33. Div. Artillery with DAC (less B. Echeln), and M.Q. Coy Divs had H.Q. transferred for Ordnance Services. Glos X.4.2 and S.4/33 T.M. Mor.	
	30		Railhead AGNEZ-LES-DUISANS	

J McDonnell Lt
D.A.D.O.S 15 Div.

(Original)

War Diary.
April. 1917.
D.A.D.O.S. 15. Div.

Vol 22

WAR DIARY / INTELLIGENCE SUMMARY

Army Form C. 2118

D.A.D.O.S. 15TH DIVISION

APRIL 1917

Place	Date	Hour	Summary of Events and Information	Remarks and references to Appendices
DUISANS	4		Receipt of Div. Arms Scout letter re establishment of Advance Gun Park PREVENT	
	5		32nd Sanitary Section transferred to O.O. XIX Corps Troops for Ordnance Services	
	9		Division went into action. Casualties to Guns, howitzers, Trench mortars and machine guns as follows:—	
	9 April		1 . 4.5" howitzer at carriage . (D/156 Bty) 1 Trench mortar 3" Stokes (45 T.M.B.)	
	10		1 18 pdr carriage (C/71)	
	11		8/10 Gordons – 5 Lewis guns	
	12		46 M.G. Co. 2 Vickers Guns	
	13		1 QF 18 pdr carriage (C/70) 1 QF 18 pdr carriage (C/70)	
	14		{4 Lewis Guns (9 Blackwatch) 1½ (11 Argylls) 3 (7/8 KOSB) 1 Vickers Guns (44 M.G.Coy)	
	15		{1 QF 18 pdr (A/70) 4 (7 Camerons)	
	16		1 QF 18 pdr carriage (A/156) 9 Lewis Guns (44 R.F.)	
	20		B Squadron 1st K.D. Gds. Wire Section 10th Research Park. Park Section Cavalry Corps Bridging Park and Cavalry Corps Signal Squadron transferred to O.O. Ordnance for Cavalry Corps	
	20		232nd Army Bde Artillery BSR transferred to Ordnance from 50th Division	
	20		33rd Divisional Artillery transferred to Ordnance Services fr. 17th Division	
	21		No 4 P.O.W Co transferred to O.O. Third Army Troops fr Ordnance	
	21		Park Section, Cavalry Corps Bridging Park transferred to 2nd Cavalry Div. fr Ordnance	

Re-equipment of Division: — IV was found that very few Steel helmets, rifles or box respirators were lost in operation; a great number of important technical stores such as Lewis Gun equipment, magazines and Very Pistols were deficient. This an individual replace

War Diary Vol 23
for
co. A.
1917.

D. a. G. Q. G. 15 D. I.

DADOS 15 Div

WAR DIARY
INTELLIGENCE SUMMARY

MAY. 1917

Army Form C. 2118.

Place	Date	Hour	Summary of Events and Information	Remarks and references to Appendices
DUISANS	4		184' Tunnelling Coy transferred to 17' Corps Troops for Ordnance Services.	
	5		1' Lincoln and 2' Middlesex Labour Coys transferred for Ordnance Services to me.	
	7		15'D.A. and 232' Army F.A. Bde transferred for Ordnance to 56' Div. - all other attached units to 29' Div.	
	8		Moved to LE CAUROY. Under XVIII Corps for administration for this date. —	
LE CAUROY	9		(Railhead SAULTY.) XVIII Corps provided us with clothing, boots + S.D. clothing from Corps "Pool". - Very useful (Railhead WARLINCOURT)	
	20			
	21		Moved to Frévent WILLEMAN, - under XIX Corps for administration. (Railhead FRÉVENT.)	
	22			
WILLEMAN	22		47' Field Amb' transferred back for Ordnance from 56 Div.	
	24		Notifications received that intimates for stores in sections 14,15,16A,17,18 for Artillery and T. M. batteries on 4' be sent to Cerans at 15 midnight 27' inst'. (Except Gun-Barrel Stores). XIX Corps ADOS 4/5/14/7 24/5/17	
	26		15'. Div'. Artillery and N° 1 Coy. Train rejoin Division from 56 Division. Above appeal to have been very badly looked after in 56'. Div'. as regards ordnance. A very large number of stores required to complete.	

Jeffrey... Lieut Col
DADOS 15 Div.

Vol 24
War Diary.
JUNE. 1917.
D.A.D.O.S 15 Div.

Original

Army Form C. 2118.

WAR DIARY

D.A.D.O.S. INTELLIGENCE SUMMARY. JUNE, 1917.
15th DIVN.

(Erase heading not required.)

Place	Date	Hour	Summary of Events and Information	Remarks and references to Appendices
WILLEMAN	1		Great difficulty in obtaining service char parts from Base. This reported to Base by wire.	
	9		Division came under Third Army orders for administration from midnight 9/10 June. — reads 30 Div. then the 1st Division in indent.	
	10		Considerable improvement during past week in supply of gun parts & fm Park.	
	14		Store stopped on both Bases until further notice.	
	15			
	16		Transferred to XIV Corps for Ordnance. (This Amendment E.O./389. 15/6/17.) Dif: Willing and 46th Bn L. have no Munts arry Division, also Pioneer Batt.	
	18		Moved by road to VLAMERTINGHE, 4 miles E. of POPERINGHE. Railhead WIPPENHOEK.	
VLAMER-TINGHE	25		Under Fifth Army and XIX Corps for administration.	
			216 Div. Employment Coy formed. (Pte INNES 7/8 K.O.S.B. Transferred to W.I.)	
	27		Ordnance Railhead POPERINGHE. Ft GARDNER. O. I/C Mobs. ditto.	
			Shortage of rubber sprays esp. for Goggles - but supply improved with charge of Base.	
	28		Demonstration at D.H.Q. of the "Yukon" Pack - 250 demands from Base.	
			Shortage of Service Chart parts - from Bases - all through the month. Also of cable for staining tents. Bar has attacks on supply wanted him.	
			Jefferson Major	
			DADOS 15 Div.	

30/6/17.

War Diary
July

DADOS 15 DIV

WAR DIARY
INTELLIGENCE SUMMARY

Army Form C. 2118.

DADOS 15 DIV

JULY/17

Place	Date	Hour	Summary of Events and Information	Remarks and references to Appendices
VLAMERTINGHE		6	Co' who revised re installation of 3i/M Army Gun Park – open 7/8th June. 1917	
		7	1/5.A. Hawy. and X.Y. 2/5.A. Medium T.M. Btys. transferred for Ordnance from 5th Australian Div	
		8	2 9.45', our staff on Inf. T.M. drawn from G.P.K.	
		9	16: Div. Artillery and No 1 Cd 16 Div. Div. attached for Ordnance Services.	
		11	16: R.D. Switches + 47 mfg Coy transferred for Ordnance from 16: DIV	
		16	Notification received that No 225 mfg Coy is no longer formed of HAVRE and will be attached 15 DIV as from M.G.Coy.	
		16	5th Australian Div Artillery, D.A.C. and 10 Coy (M.I Section) A/A.S.C. transferred for Ordnance to O.O. XIX Corps troops for Ordnance. (Auth: XIX Corps SQ/114/3)	
		17	16 R.D. Switches transferred to O.O. XIX Corps Troops for Ordnance	
		19	Arrival of 225 Machine Gun Company.	
			Remarks. 2 parts	
			Supply from 3i/M Army Ordnance Sup. Park very fair – much letter than Third Army. On the whole have spoken of supplies as much mv & satisfactory from one point of view, as information as to supplies no not often supplies arrive late.	
			Complaints made of large numbers of Box Mophiches Extracins arriving broken far Base. R This spoils force – about 20%.	
31/9/17				J.H.Critchley G DADOS 15 Div

D.A.D.O.S.
15th Division.

War Diary
August 1917

Army Form C. 2118.

DADOS. 15 Division WAR DIARY
or
INTELLIGENCE SUMMARY. AUGUST 1917

Vol 26

Place	Date	Hour	Summary of Events and Information	Remarks and references to Appendices
VLAMER-TINGHE	3		5th Australian D.A. and 10 Coy Aust. A.S.C., 16 D.A. and No 1 Coy 16 Div Train and 47 N.S. Coy transferred to DADOS 16 Div. ft Ordnance Service	I.
	4		Moved to WINNIZEELE. Railhead WIPPENHOEK	I.
WINNIZEELE			Losses of Division in operations 31st July to 3rd August. — 82 hus guns + 2 subsequents enquired. 13 Vickers guns + 4 Lewis guns captured. 7 Stokes mortars. Replacing of stores. Rem Base at Gen Park supplied 13 rifles + rod	I. I. I. I. I/6 I/6
	18		Moved back to VLAMERTINGHE. (H.7.t.11). Railhead Poperinghe.	I/6 I/6
	18		5 Australian D.A. complete and 16: D.A. complete transferred back to Ordnance from DADOS 16 Div.	I/7
VLAMERTINGHE			Losses of Division in operations 22nd August. 34 Lewis guns, 3 Vickers — 6 huns, 5 Vickers upsmith in addition to Ammunition dump. No mortars lost.	I/7
	28		5 Australian D.A., D.A.C, T.n. Bhp and No 10 Coy Aust M.C. transferred to 42: Division	I/6 I/6
	28		Calais PM 16 transfer ordinarily instructs for unit to Div 15 Southern Base	I/6 I/6
	31		Moved to WATOU. Railhead WIPPENHOEK. 42: Div Ordnance taking on Ordnance Dumps at VLAMERTINGHE.	I/7

31/8/17

Ed Cruickshank Capt
DADOS 15 Div.

No 27

War Diary
for
September 1917
DADOS 15 Div

WAR DIARY

INTELLIGENCE SUMMARY.

DADOS 15. DIVISION

SEPTEMBER 1917

Army Form C. 2118.

Place	Date	Hour	Summary of Events and Information	Remarks and references to Appendices
WATOU	2		{ Moved by road to HERMAVILLE (called AGNEZ-LES-DUISANS. Under 3rd Army and XVII Corps for administration.	
HERMAVILLE	5.		6662. T/Cpl. (a/S/Sjt(md)) KIRKHAM tried by F.G.C.M. on 29th July for Drunkenness, found guilty and sentenced to 28 days D[eprivation of] pay. — sentence promulgated on 5/9/17.	
	7		Railhd ARRAS.	
	8.		Moved to ARRAS.	
ARRAS	9	9.45	Lorry halts. T.M. drawn from Ord. and SunPark and DDOS 0/50/49 3/9/17	
	11	10.00	10.00 Blankets returned for Disinfection in Fumerie.	
	17		Dept visited by Major General Sir J Steevens KCB, DEOS, C.A. DOS. and Major General A DE PREE DMS.	
	28	4	New MR 6° T.M.Mos drawn from Ord. and SunPark as hand over to D.T.M.O.	
	28		Lieut. C.W. WIGGINS A.O.D. arrived for duty.	

Signed,
DADOS 15 Div.
31/9/17

Vol 28.

War Diary

OCTOBER. 1917.

Army Form C. 2118.

WAR DIARY
INTELLIGENCE SUMMARY

(Erase heading not required.)

DADOS 15th Division

OCTOBER 1917

Instructions regarding War Diaries and Intelligence Summaries are contained in F.S. Regs., Part II. and the Staff Manual respectively. Title pages will be prepared in manuscript.

Place	Date	Hour	Summary of Events and Information	Remarks and references to Appendices
ARRAS.	1		No. 19 Train Crew Section attached for Ordnance Services	
	6		1 Section of 225 M.G. Coy left Division.	
	19		'Second blankets' received in full from Base	
	22		Leather jerkins & undercoats received for Inf'y only from Base	
	22		Third Army Tramways Coy transferred for Ordnance Services to 16th Div.	
	23		265 Area Employment Coy, New Zealand Engineer Tunnelling Coy RE, 6th and 25th Antiaircraft Searchlight Sections RE transferred for Ordnance Services from 12th Division	
	26		6847 Pte HUNTER P. 1st Gordon Hldrs and 260149 Pte THOMSON P. 5th Gordon Hldrs (T.F.) arriving from ETAPLES for duty with Ordnance. (Arm Class B men)	
	29		265 Area Employment Coy transferred to 61st Div'n for Ordnance Services	
	30		6847 Pte HUNTER P. & Gordons & 260149 Pte THOMSON P. 5th Gordons A.D.D.M. 46 Div. (17 Corps were O/C 31.9.17 (Infantry)	
7-30?			Lt. FIELD, A.O.D, inspecting armourers, inspected machine guns and rifles of Division	
	31		3000 pairs of Gum Boots received from Base, making total of 5000 pairs kept in charge of Division.	
	31/10/17			

[Signature]
DADOS 15th Div

Vol 29

War Diary.

D.A.D.O.S. 15th Division

NOVEMBER 1917.

DADOS 15 Division WAR DIARY
INTELLIGENCE SUMMARY. NOVEMBER 1917.

Army Form C. 2118.

Place	Date	Hour	Summary of Events and Information	Remarks and references to Appendices
ARRAS.	1		Pte REID. A.O.C. genl instruction in repairs to Gun Parts to run 5th & 7th from units of Divn.	E
	7		0/4158 – Pt S.V. THOMPSON efy to proceed to Base, HAVRE	E
	8		25th Anti-Aircraft Searchlight Section transferrer to O/C VIII Corps Troops	E
	9		A Special Coy. R.E. joins from O.C. II Corps Troops for Ordnance	E
	10		Lieut C.W. WIGGINS. A.O.D. refr to proceed to Base, ROUEN	E
	14		31st Army Tramway Co. R.E. transferred to 24th Divn for Ordnance Services	E
	14		70 Bde R.F.A. (all units) transferred to 51st Divn for Ordnance Services	E
	15		70 Bde R.F.A. transferred to 51st Div. to O.O. IV Corps Troops for Ordnance	E
	18		N.1 Section 15 D.A.C. transferred to O.O. 4th Corps Troops for Ordnance	E
	20		N.2 Army Tramway Coy R.E. transferred to O.O. 15th Corps Troops for Ordnance	E
	26		N.3 Special Coy (Igniters) R.E. transferred from 34th Division for Ordnance Services	E
	26		B.Coy 5th Canadian Railway Construction Bn. transferred from Ordnance VI Corps Troops for Ordnance Services	E
	28		HdQrs 61st D.A, HQ 307, 131 R.F.A, A.B.C. v D Bats 307 R 131 R.F.A, X.Y.Z. n Sm. T.M.B's 4/61 Hvy.T.M.B'Y, 61st D.A.C transferred from 61st Divn for Ordnance Service	E
	30		M.L.Cg 61st Divn v N.61 A.S.P. transferred from 61st Division for Ordnance Service	E
	30		N.6 Anti-Aircraft Searchlight Section transferred to O.O. II Corps Troops for Ordnance	E

[signature]
DADOS 15th Division

War Diary.

December 1917.

D.A.D.O.S. 15th Division.

Volume 2. No. 12.

WAR DIARY

INTELLIGENCE SUMMARY. D.A.D.O.S. 15TH DIVISION.

DECEMBER 1917

Army Form C. 2118.

Place	Date	Hour	Summary of Events and Information	Remarks and references to Appendices
ARRAS	8		No 1 Section 61st DAC transferred to 5th Corps Troops No 2 Siege Park	
	11		13 Coy 5th Canadian Rly Construction Bn. moved to 5 Corps to join remainder of Batt.	
	12		No 3093, A/Cpl. T. Davies sent back to his Batt. (9th Gordon Highlanders)	
	12		HQ 61st D.A. transferred to 61st Division for Ordnance.	
	14		12th Bde Canadian Railway Troops transferred for Ordnance from 3rd Division.	
	15		X.Y.Z/61 Medium and V/61 Heavy T.M. Btys transferred to Ordnance from 15 DADOS 61st Div.	
	16		"A" Special Coy, R.E. and No 3 Special Coy, R.E. transferred to Ordnance to DADOS, G.H.Q. Troops	
	17		C/71 Bde R.F.A. transferred for Ordnance from 00 Divl/Army Troops No 2	
	17		HQ 61st DAC transferred to DADOS 61st Div for Ordnance	
	19		SAA Section 61 DAC transferred to DADOS 61st Div for Ordnance	
	20		70 Bigade MMG transferred for Ordnance from DADOS 9th Division	
	22		307 Brigade RFA, No 2 Sec. 61 DAC, M.I.Coy 61 Divl Train, 61 Amn Sub Park transferred	
	23		to DADOS 61st Divn for Ordnance service.	
	24		No 1 Subsection 15 DAC transferred from 00 V Corps Troops for Ordnance	
	27		Extra Gun Park Stores to be drawn in future from Advanced Army Gun Park BAPAUME	

John Clark
DADOS 15th Division

Confidential   VA.32

War Diary
of
S.A.S.O.S. 15th Division

From 1/2/18   To 28/2/18

FEBRUARY 1918 WAR DIARY

Army Form C. 2118.

INTELLIGENCE SUMMARY. D.A.D.O.S. 15TH DIVISION

(Erase heading not required.)

Place	Date	Hour	Summary of Events and Information	Remarks and references to Appendices
MEAS.	1		No. 26382 Pte T. O'ROURKE 12th H.L.I. reports his return indst instructions 15 Divl "A"	h
	2		12th H.L.I. transferred to DADOS 35 Divn for Ordnance Services	h
	7		1st Line & Train transport of 11th K.O.R. Lanc Regt arrived from 40 Divn & attached to 46 Bde	h
	8		Indent submitted on S. Park for 29 Lewis guns & equipments & A.A. work in accordance with QMG 53/10 (QNS) 4.2.18. (18 for Instructing [2 per Bn], 3 for R.E. Field Cpy & 1 Div. Cyc. Coy 8TH)	h
	8		12th Bn Canadian Railway Troops transferred to OIC 7th Corps Troops for Ordnance	h
	11		8 Lewis guns received (for Mattresses RM4 – 1 each) from Gun Park under Army 53/10 (QNS3) 4.2.18	h
	12		S/16662 L/Cpl. KIRKHAM A.O.C. relinquished acting rank of S/Sgt (Gun Instr) and left for duty under C.O.O. HAVRE. (Authority Third Army O/4/147. 4.2.18.)	h
	15		Lr. W. JENKIN. A⋅O⋅D reported for duty – under Order Third Army C/458 13/7/17 · 15/2/18	h
	16		18 Lewis guns received (for Battle 2 per Bn) from G. Park under Order 53/10 (QNS3) 4.2.18	h
	16		Rt 0/21165 S/Sgnt A.J. THOMAS posted for duty are from 11/2/18 (A.M. 3rd Army O/4/147)	h
	17		No. 260149 Pte P. THOMSON 5 Gordon Hdrs. transferred to A.O.C. & form reqt No. 036555 from 31/1/17 Auth. D.A.G. 3rd Army C.R. 32007/1/155	h
	18		V/15 Heavy T.M.B. absorbed into V/XVII Corps Heavy T.M.B. Means rels. etc. (XVII Corps Q/R/33 17/M/18)	h
	18		1st Line + Train Transport of 23rd Bn Manchesters Regt arrived & attached to 45 Bde	h

A6945 Wt. W11422/M1160 350,000 12/16 D.D.&I. Forms/C./2118/14.

DADOS 15 Divison

WAR DIARY
of
INTELLIGENCE SUMMARY.
(Erase heading not required.)

February 1918

Army Form C. 2118.

Place	Date	Hour	Summary of Events and Information	Remarks and references to Appendices
ARRAS	21		47 Cycl. Sub. Section moved to 50. Divison	E
	22		Following units of 158. A.F.A. Bde. proceeded to rail head for Ordnance Service. H.Q. 158th A.F.A.Bde, 241st Brigade Ammn Column, B Battery R.H.A., 380th Battery R.F.A. (B/158-152 A.F.A.), 241st Berkshire Battery R.F.A. (C/158-152 A.F.A.), 380th Battery R.F.A. (D/158-152 A.F.A.) 158th Brigade Ammn Column	E
	24		16 Lewis Guns received (for Field Companies R.E. and N.Z. Eng Tunnelling Co - 1 each) from Gun Park under Q.M.G. S/ho (R.83) 4-2-18	H.
	26		34 Lewis Guns received to complete Batteries (including A.F.A attached) and regimentally under Auth. Q.M.G. S/ho R.83 of 16.2.18	H.
	27		Machine Gun Companies re-organised into Machine Gun Battalion 1/3/18	H.

A. Hendersin Lieut
for Captain
A.A.S.O.S. 15th Division

WA 33

D.A.D.O.S. 15th Division

War Diary.
March 1918.

WAR DIARY
INTELLIGENCE SUMMARY

March 1918 DADOS 15 Division

Army Form C. 2118.

Place	Date	Hour	Summary of Events and Information	Remarks and references to Appendices
ARRAS	10		15 Div. Supply Column amalgamated with N° 15 A.S.C. to form N° 15 Div. M.T. Co.	
	11		1 15 pr Anti-Tank gun received by Division	
	15		Capt J.G. MISSENDEN, DADOS attached to 17 Corps.	
	18		15 Bat.M.G. Corps formed from 44, 45, 46 & 128 Machine Gun Coys	
	22		Raided and KAGNEZ LES DUISANS	
	21	0/2495	L/Corp. BAYNHAM E. and 0/2440 Pt. LADE E. wounded during bombardment of ARRAS Both taken	
			to N°7 C.C.S. Pt. LADE died of wounds 21/22nd inst. L/C BAYNHAM evacuated to Base.	
	23		Ordnance Dump moved to WARLUS	
WARLUS	24-26		Units refund all surplus stores which are sent to Base at once	
	26		N°7 Mobile Workshop Store attached for Ordnance	
	26		Dump moved to AGNEZ L DUISANS	
	26		6 Lewis Guns & Spare parts reiss'd on being in lieu to "Divisional Reserve" = 3 Lewis	
			Guns issued to M.G. Batt. held distribution of ADOS	
	31		20 L. Guns drawn for from Bab AUXI LE CHATEAU	

DADOS 15 Div.

WAR DIARY. - M APRIL, 1918.

D.A.D.O.S. 15th DIVISION.

Army Form C. 2118

DADOS 15th Division WAR DIARY
INTELLIGENCE SUMMARY
APRIL 1918

(Erase heading not required.)

Place	Date	Hour	Summary of Events and Information	Remarks and references to Appendices
MARLUS.	2		No. 2 Army Stores Coy. R.E. Transferred to 9th Corps Troops	
	3		Leave in action 21/3/18 to 1/4/18. Vickers Guns complete 39 with approx. 880 belts & boxes	
			Lewis Guns. 7 Cameron. 18. 9th Gordons 8. = 26	
			13 R. Scots 12 6 Cameron 10 = 22	
			9 M. Lancs 6 7/8 KOSB 3 = 9	
			R.A. C/71. 1 - D/158. 2 B/70..2 = 6	
			63	
			Magazines - approximately 2000.	
			Trench mortars - Stokes 3". - 44. T.M.B. - 8	
			45 T.M.B. - 6	
			46 T.M.B. - 2	
			16	
	7		23rd Marshals Regt v 11 KORL Regt (Graphic Infantry Draveports) withdrawn from Division to join 5th Reserve Bde	
	7		Under Army for administration. All intents transferred to CALAIS.	
	10		Ordnance Issue Park intents transferred to N.1 Gun Park	
	11		Lt. W. JENKIN left for duty as D.A.D.O.S. 55th Division. (17 Corps O.O 314 11.4.18)	
	11		158. A.F.A. Bde transferred to I Corps Troops	
	13		No. 6/30330 Pte DUFFIN. F. (Storeman) A.O.C. as No. 19/869 Pte ANDERSON. W. (Clerk) 11th R.I. Rifles arrives from Base for duty. (D.A.G. O.C. 823. 25.3.18)	
	13		Lt. Div. Artillery, (two S.Q.M. Sergts DAE), and No. 1 Coy 4th Div Train Transferred to O.C. Train. S/Conr LEECH, A.O.C. and 2 Storemen joined for duty with above from DADOS 4. Div	

Army Form C. 2118.

WAR DIARY
INTELLIGENCE SUMMARY.
(Erase heading not required.)

Place	Date	Hour	Summary of Events and Information	Remarks and references to Appendices
WARLUS	15		M.T. Workshops & Squadron transferred to L. of C. Artisans transferred to D.D.O.S. 15 Army	
	16		3 Surplus Cooks Carts to 15 I.O. M.G. Coys returned to Dour. AGNEZ Trucks 44021 (2) 51534 (1) W.B. CP 610 B.II. 13 to 15	
	17		Store Arm. G.S. 22/34 14/4/18. Bolt. programmes on Calais route.	
	18		H.Q. 4th D. Amm Col. all units of 32nd Bdell F.A transferred to DADOS 4th Division	
	19		N.1 Section 4th D.A.C. transferred to DADOS 4th Div.	
	22		Remnil of 4th D.A. units and N.1 Coy 4th Div Train Transferred to DADOS 4 Div.	
	23		HQ 15 DA 7th, 71 DLI, 9/R. H.R. & N.F. 1.2 Section DAC X/15 Y/15 TM.Bty, M.G. Coy Train Transferred to DADOS 15 Div for administration	
	23		New Zealand Tunnelling Coy R.E. Transferred to OD 17 Corps Troops	
	24		HQrs to AUCHEL Under XIII Corps for administration	
AUCHEL	26		(Railed) LILLERS	
	30		Picric acid authorised to H.Q 12 Divisions. Order 8003/14 (Q.C.1) 29/4/18	

30/4/18

[signature]
DADOS 15th DIVISION

WAR DIARY

MAY 1918.

D.A.D.O.S. 15th DIVISION.

D.A.D.O.S. 15th DIVISION

WAR DIARY
INTELLIGENCE SUMMARY
MAY. 1918.

Army Form C. 2118.

Place	Date	Hour	Summary of Events and Information	Remarks and references to Appendices
AUCHEL	1		Pte DUFFIN. F. A.D.C. sent to O.C. XI Corps Troops for duty (auth: D.D.o.S. 3rd Army OS 10/7/91)	
	4		Moved to AGNEZ LES DUISANS under XVII Corps for administration	28.4.18
AGNEZ-DUISANS	5		Reached AGNEZ LES DUISANS	
	5		15. D.A. Transferred back to me for Ordnance for 56 Divn (G.H/Rs/23)	
	5		2nd Divl Artillery (HQ - HQ 36th 136 CFA 15", 48", 91" and D/36 (HH) DACs, HQ 41st Row NBA, 9", 16", 17" & 47" (CHT) RAS, 1. X/2, Y/2 HQ. T.M Bde, HQ 2nd DAC with Nº1, 2 Sections, 1 Sg 2nd Bn Divnl Transferred to Ordnance Services from 1st Canadian Divn	
	7		S/Cpl. DALLY . Pte STURDY reported for duty with 2nd D.A. from 1st Canadian Divn	
	8		6 Lewis Guns received to complete Pioneer Battn to 12 under Auth: QMG 8003/14 (QC1) 25/4/18	
	14		4/5 Bn Royal Highlanders transferred for 39 Divn to Ordnance	
	15		72 Lewis Guns drawn from Ord. to complete Battns to Scale E. = 24 per Bn. (1st Army OS 2040 g 14/5/18)	
	22		S/Cpl. DALLY now btd. to 2nd Divn - replaced by S/Cpl. CHANEY. A.O.C.	
	25		Nº 1 (1st Life Guards) Battn Machine Gun Guards attached for Ordnance - (arms for Base) Corps Troops	
	26		16 surplus Hotchkiss Lewis Guns withdrawn from 4/5 B.Watch & sent to Gun Park	
	29		"Cadre" Battn 9 Black Watch transferred to DADOS 39 Divn	

J.M.Crichton Capt
DADOS 15 Divn
31/5/18

WAR DIARY FOR JUNE, 1918.

D.A.D.O.S. 15th DIVISION.

JUNE 1918   WAR DIARY   DADOS 15th DIV   Army Form C. 2118.
or
INTELLIGENCE SUMMARY.
(Erase heading not required.)

Place	Date	Hour	Summary of Events and Information	Remarks and references to Appendices
AGNEZ-LES DUISANS	1			
	1		0/30330 Pte DUFFIN F. Att'd typist of Duty to OO XI Corps Troops	1/6
	1		1/A Royal Scots. 1/5 Gordon Highlanders on A/c Supply Sub. Mob. into Division fr 61st Division	1/6
	8		1/5 Gordon Hdrs absorbs 8/10 Gordon Hdrs - New Div reference title ⅔ 1/5 Gordon Hdrs.	1/6
	9		1/6 Argyll & Suth. Hders absorb 11 A & S Hdrs. New Div reference title ⅔ 11/8 A & S Hdrs.	1/6
	9		"Capt" NAIT-(Training Instr.) ⅔ 9th Gordons, 11 Argylls & 7 Camerons "joined" fr DADOS 39th Div.	1/6
	10		6 M.G. Coys Hdrs attached 7: M.G. Camerons Hdrs, retaining title of 6 Cameron Hdrs:	1/6
	14		3/6 Cam. Hdrs complete with equipt S/&4 magazine Rifles fr 51st Division	1/6
	19		2: Div. Artillery complete on O/C 2: Div C.R.A. transferred fr DADOS 2nd Div. to C.R.A. ours.	1/6
	22		S/Capt. CHANEY and Lt. STURDY post to DADOS 2: Div.	1/6
	22		Division continues to be complete in Scale "F" in Lewis Guns (complete fr 26 pr. Pack or dismt?) 1st Army O.S. 8/249 4/6/18	1/6
	25/27		Division complete to Scale "F" (28 guns per Battn) fr Lewis Guns. Ene anti-aircraft	1/6
	30		0/2589 2/Capt. KNOWLES H. sent to M.T. Ordnance by Mil Workshops (Heavy) to duty as Sup Clerk (Auth DDOS 3rd Army O.S. 10/071 28/6/18)	1/6

Jno Zimmerman Major
DADOS 15th Div

WAR DIARY.
D.A.D.O.S. 15th DIVN.
JULY. 1918

WAR DIARY or INTELLIGENCE SUMMARY

Army Form C. 2118.

DADOS 15th Division

Vol 37

JULY 1918

Place	Date	Hour	Summary of Events and Information	Remarks and references to Appendices
AGNEZ-DUISANS	5		Major J.G. HIBBERT, DADOS proceeded on leave to U.K.	
	7		1 extra Vickers gun authorised for training to each M.G.Bn. (Div Army. O.S.8/269 6/7/18)	
	7		4 extra Lewis guns authorised for A.A. purposes to each Inf. Bn. (Div Army. O.S.8/269) 6.7.18	
	7		O/22950 Pte CLENNELL, A.O.C. arrived for duty.	
	12		No.1 (1st Life Guards) Bn. M.G. Guards Transferred to D.O. Canadian Corps Troops for Ordnance	
	14		Moved to FREVIN-CAPELLE. (called FREVIN CAPELLE)	
FREVIN-CAPELLE	15		Transferred to XVII Corps to Southern Area.	
	16		Moved to BRYAS.	
BRYAS	17		Entrained at BRYAS.	
	18		Detrained at LIANCOURT, marching LIANCOURT by road	
LIANCOURT	19		To PIERREFONDS	
PIERREFONDS	20		To GUISE LAMOTTE	
GUISE LAMOTTE	22		To VIVIERES {Under XX French Corps for administration. 'Q' (GHQ (S) attached to CRCN D.H.Q. at COEUVRES. Railhead MORIENVAL	
VIVIERES	23		No.2 O.M.W.(L) established at L'EPINE FARM. 1½ Miles N. of VIVIERES.	
	24		Major J.G. HIBBERT returned. in latter transferred on 27 July to O.O. CRCN	
	22		No.37 M.A.C. and 63rd C.C.S. arrived in Area. Started to on for Ordnance Services	
	29		Railhead from Lanza to VILLERS-COTTERETS.	

JADOS 15th Division

War Diary.
AUGUST 1918
D.A.D.O.S. 15th DIVN.

WAR DIARY
DADOS 15th DIVISION
AUGUST 1918 INTELLIGENCE SUMMARY

Army Form C. 2118.

No. 38

Place	Date	Hour	Summary of Events and Information	Remarks and references to Appendices
VIVIÈRES	1		Losses in actn of Vickers & Lewis Guns :- 1 Vickers taken for 3 mos entrenchd	
			Lewis Guns :- 8 Septrs -16, 1/8 Argylls - 4, 7/8 KOSB - 19, 9/5 Mid Wilts - 9 1/5 Gordons 1	
			6 Cameron 3, 11/Scot Rif 8	
			Trench Mortars 4.4 T.M.B. - 4.	
	4		Moved by road to LIANCOURT. Large consignment of M.F.G. for Tanks picked up en route.	
LIANCOURT	6		Moved by road to AMBRINES (160 Kilometres). Under XXII (British) Corps for administration	
AMBRINES	8		Railway TINCQUES	
	12		Lt EVETT A.O.D. Inspecting of Ordnance, Divn Army, visits Ordnance Shops	
	14		Grant shelter & soap et. equipment owing to no receipt of Rear Reports to DDOS.	
	16		Moved to MONTENESCOURT relieving DADOS 56 Divn. Under XVII Corps ft administration	
MONTENESCOURT	18		Railway AGNEZ-LES-DUISANS	
	18		309 Amern M.G 182 311 M.G Coy, 1" B. 3" R.A.F. 3/11 Arct Regt A.E.F returng 66	
			Vickers & 106 Lewis Guns & equipment	
	(23		S. A.A. Indry Instructing XVII Corps	
	(20		15 DA & No 1 Coy Divn moved to DADOS 2nd Canadian Div for Ordnance Services	
	25		D.D.O.S. Divn Army visited	
			Railway BARLIN	
BRAQUEMONT	26		Moved to BRAQUEMONT taking on from DADOS 11" Divn. Under I Corps ft administrn	

WAR DIARY (Continued)
or
INTELLIGENCE SUMMARY. DADOS 15th Division

Army Form C. 2118.

Month: August 18

Place	Date	Hour	Summary of Events and Information	Remarks and references to Appendices
YSMAQUEMONT.				
	30		11th D.A. (less S.A.A. Section + A Nos. 58 RSS 17A) Transferred for Ordnance for 11th Division	
	30		Lt. Timms. A.O.D. inspects Boot Shops + Bath - Dir. Shoemaker Shop	

D.A.D.O.S.
15TH DIVISION.
Date 31/8/18

Jenkins Major
DADOS 15th Division

WO 39

War Diary
for September 1918
D.A.D.O.S. 15 Division

WAR DIARY
INTELLIGENCE SUMMARY

DADOS 15th DIVISION.

SEPTEMBER 1918

Army Form C. 2118

Place	Date	Hour	Summary of Events and Information	Remarks and references to Appendices
BLAQUEMONT	1		Held Conference of all Quartermasters. On Supply. No complaints, except as regards shortage of yellow soap. Applied to ADOS for a hair's brush.	
	4		S/Capt THOMAS. Pte ANDERSON transferred to Co. XXII Corps Troops for duty with 15 D.A. Details from 2. (Canadian) Div. (D.A.D.o.S. 2 Can. Div. F 29/3/2/28 4.9.18.)	
	7		15th D.A. & N° 1 Cy Train returns from XXII Corps. Arrival confirmed to Base (GH.39).	
	7		H.Q. H.D.A., H.Q. "D.A.C." N° 1.2 Sections. H.Q. "A" B.C. "D" B'y S.Q. B.D.'s R'y.A. H.Q. "B.C."D"B'y (GH.40).	
			58th Bde. R.F.A. X/11, Y/11 T.M.B.'s & N° 1 C of 11th Div. R'ns and to DADoS 11th Div. Dinr.	
	9		02685 ¾ Sgt REECH B. & 0/36524 Pt GORDY P. returning to DADOS 11th Divn.	
	12		2 hand guns pr Batters RfA for ground defence instructs for (Auth DDOS O.B/249 - 19.7.18)	
	19		I Corps transferred to Fifth Army for administration.	
	26		DDOS Fifth Army visited by Damp.	
			Remarks:- General shortage of Soap, soda and paint stores - supplies of the 2 first items being only received in full as & to last week of prospective Omnium. Supplies sent - Havlours sent for horse clippers & apparatus spotphrodes illuminating.	

B.A.D.O.S. XV DIVn

30 SEP 1918

WAR DIARY

OCTOBER. 1918.

DADOS. 15th DIVISION.

DADOS, 15th Division WAR DIARY
or
INTELLIGENCE SUMMARY.   October 1918.

Place	Date	Hour	Summary of Events and Information	Remarks and references to Appendices
BRAQUEMONT	6		Railhead transferred from BARLIN to NOEUX-LES-MINES	F
	8		M2609 Orr. S/Sergt SINCLAIR admission place of An S/Sgt ILSLEY evacuated sick	F
	15		Additional 4 Lewis Guns per Inft. Bn. (to complete to full scale (Scale 'G') of 32 ordinary plus 4 A.A. guns sanctioned by Sd. War Army GA 291/44 of 11th instant	F
	18		Move to CARVIN. Rear Group H.Q. in BRAQUEMONT.	F
CARVIN	19		Move to THUMERIES Dump 2 with store not immediately required up at CARVIN	F
THUMERIES	20		Move to CAPELLE Stores shipped on Barges 36 ordinary Lewis Guns returned	F
CAPELLE	20		31/N Army Gun Pork WAZIERS	F
	21		158 A.F.A. Bde attached for O.S. now same	F
	21		Move to GENECH. Now back to Bdes for all remainder 15th Div. Stores	F
GENECH	23		Railhead changed to MARQUILLIES	F
	24		Blanket Store (British/American) working distribution opened at Ch. VIEL A.D.08	F
	25		Move to LA GLANERIE. No. 6 Ordnance Workshops now here TEMPLEUVE No 15 at CARVIN	F
LA GLANERIE	26		Railhead → DON	F
			Great difficulty experienced in obtaining with supplies owing to bad roads & distances	F

J.H. Brown Major
DADOS 15th Div
31.10.18

CONFIDENTIAL.

WAR DIARY OF

D.A.D.O.S. 15th (SCOTTISH) DIVISION.

FROM NOVEMBER 1st 1918. TO NOVEMBER 30th, 1918.

VOLUME.

Army Form C. 2118

WAR DIARY
or
INTELLIGENCE SUMMARY   D.A.D.O.S 15th Divn
(Erase heading not required.)

NOVEMBER 1918

Place	Date	Hour	Summary of Events and Information	Remarks and references to Appendices
LA GLANERIE	2		Railhead changed from DON to LILLE.	1/11
	9		Moved to WEZ-VELVAIN. Dump left at LA GLANERIE.	2/11
WEZ	10		Moved to ANTOING. Railhead changed to FRETIN.	3/11
ANTOING	11		Crossed the SCHELDT canal and moved to TOURPES.	4/11
TOURPES	13		15 Divn transferred to III Corps for administration.	5/11
	14		Railhead changed from FRETIN to BAISIEUX.	6/11
	17		Moved to ORMEIGNIES.	7/11
ORMEIGNIES	18-30		All principal articles of winter clothing issued.	
			Remarks:- Great difficulty experienced by instructors after having been visited by Corps had all surplus equipment in possession made steady & stamped Base - no subsequent instructions than this have not to be done - Supplies from Base seeming to much - very good.	

1/12/18.

[signature]
D.A.D.O.S. 15th Division

War Diary

D.A.D.O.S. 15th Division

Period:— Dec: 1st 1918 to Dec: 31st 1918.

Volume No. Unknown

D.A.D.O.S. WAR DIARY

15th Divn. INTELLIGENCE SUMMARY. DECEMBER 1918

Army Form C. 2118.

Vol 42

Place	Date	Hour	Summary of Events and Information	Remarks and references to Appendices
ORMEIGNIES	3		No. 0/36555 Pte P. THOMSON sent for temporary duty with 1 O.M. N & 3 O.M. Workshops Motors under instructions of A.D.O.S. III Corps	
	12		Railhead changed from RAISIEUX to ATH	
	16		Railhead changed from ATH to GHISLENGHIEN	
	16		Moved to BRAINE LE CHATEAU. Railhead changed from GHISLENGHIEN to HAL	
BRAINE LE CHATEAU	20		2 Lund Gun complete returned from our 13/6 RFA under O.D./215 9/12/18 returned to Calais	
	26		No. S.14195 Pte WILSON. 415 B.W.W. left for Dunkirk as a civilian.	
	29		No. 22050 Pte J. CLENNELL R.A.O.C. left for Dunkirk as a civilian.	
	31		Sent in an official report on delays in supply of Boots for Base V.G.O.C. Divn	
			Remarks :—	
			Supplies from Base very erratic — and trucks taken a long time to reach Railhead for Base. A lot of trouble with the Clothing Group at Base — several carriers receiving nothing in delay in the supply of Boots v the important stores such as Boot repairing material.	

31/12/1918

D.A.D.O.S. XV Divn

War Diary V/U

D.A.D.O.S. 15th Division.

Period Jan'y 1st – 31st, 1919.

Volume N.

Thos. De La Rue & Co. Ltd., Bunhill Row, E.C.
W3125/1706 1,200m 6/15

Forms
C. 348
―――
61

Army Form C. 348.

MEMORANDUM.

No._____

| From | From |
| To | To |

ANSWER.

_____   _____
_____191   _____191

No._____

MEMORANDUM.

WAR DIARY or INTELLIGENCE SUMMARY

Army Form C. 2118.

D.A.D.O.S. 15 Division

6 JANUARY 1919. Vol 4

Place	Date	Hour	Summary of Events and Information	Remarks and references to Appendices
BRAINE LE CHATEAU	1		Weekly report to A.A. & Q.M.G. on subject of delay in the shipment of Boots from Calais.	E
	8		Supplies from Bases – Ruth Stores – being period 1st to 8th very erratic and no arrival of any the same.	E
			Bullets are not automatically cancelled & the two components of Ruth Stores demanded on 2 successive weekly reports frequently arrive together in the same truck, i.e. it is the one ord stores arr 3 weeks after first originally demanded. Trucks take to dump 15 wagon	
			Railways from Base: Shirley & Boots. Dublin. Morleys. Paines, Serre, Claus, Blanchlitz, Brienne. Was Calais it send up 7 F.S. Boots if available but available for some companies.	E E
	10		Particulars of demobilization for R.A.O.C. personnel sent L.A.D.O.S. III Corps	E
	17		Went with D.A.Q.M.G. to NIVELLES to inspect German abandoned material and to discuss site for a dump for it. Captain FAYERS, R.G.A. in charge of guns at park at NIVELLES. All German wagons and equipment were in a very bad state owing to exposure & weather.	E
	19		Boots of last arrival from Base: 95% of satisfactory demands met.	E
	21		L/C M. INNES. 216 Employment Coy - 16 return to clothing, left to be demobilized under Group 10	E
	21		L/C. J.W. MURGATROYD & Pte C.L. REES. 216 Empl: Coy left with demobilized (Quinche) for Calais	E
	21		M.0/43235 Pte E. PUGH R.A.O.C. arrived to duty from Stores in place of Pte CLENNELL	E
	27		Pte E.J. MOURE. 216 Employment Coy. left to be demobilized. (Quinche L.A.R)	E

Army Form C. 2118

JANUARY 1919 WAR DIARY or INTELLIGENCE SUMMARY DADOS 15 Divisn

(Erase heading not required.)

Place	Date	Hour	Summary of Events and Information	Remarks and references to Appendices
BRAINE LE CHATEAU			Remarks:— Supplies of Bulk Stores have been drawing while weather was unsettled and unsatisfactory. No Boot Laces, hardly any Polishing material during the whole month; certain sizes of hoarshirts, namely 9 hundred, 4 hundred, 6 hundred, 7 hundred 8 fives, and sizes of boots were received not in such quantities or not at all. No Stannulette of sympa cloths received during the whole month. Shortage of papers, rubbers and soap. — Took over Lett. Mor Salving Dump of Guns returned to NIVELLES on 22nd inst. All abandoned T.M's, M.Guns and Lt. 10 M N° 13 O.M.W (L), WAUTHIER BRAINE. S/Cmdr. GRAHAM. Pt WORTHINGTON Put in charge of NIVELLES Dump.	← ←
	31/1/19			

Geth...main
DADOS 15 Divisn

Confidential

War Diary

D.A.D.O.S

15th Division

February, 1919.

Army Form C. 2118

WAR DIARY
or
INTELLIGENCE SUMMARY
(Erase heading not required.)

February 1919

D.A.D.O.S.
15TH DIVISION

Instructions regarding War Diaries and Intelligence Summaries are contained in F.S. Regs., Part II. and the Staff Manual respectively. Title Pages will be prepared in manuscript.

Place	Date	Hour	Summary of Events and Information	Remarks and references to Appendices
Brimeuse Chateau	3/2/19	—	Transfer Capt (A/Major) J.A. Hotton, M.C., R.A.O.C. — D.A.D.O.S. 15th Division, granted leave to U.K. —	✱
—	4/2/19	—	No. 0/43735 Private E.J. Pugh, R.A.O.C. left for U.K. for Demobilization —	
Taresis	14/2/19	—	No. 0/2384 Armourer Staff Sergt. W. Rhodes, R.A.O.C. (attached to Division H.Q.) left for U.K. for Demobilization —	
U.K.	19/2/19	—	✱ Temp. Captain (A/Major) J.G. Hibbert, M.C., R.A.O.C. proceeds to United Kingdom on unfit to General Service & Transferred to the Home Establishment as from 19th Feb.—	✱
Brimeuse Chateau	20/2/19	—	1/5 Battalion Gordon H'rs transferred to 62nd Division for Advance Troops —	
—	24/2/19	—	11th Northumberland Hussars Yeomanry transferred from II Corps Troops to 15th Division for Advance Troops —	
—	27/2/19	—	Captain J.T. Groves-O'Sullivan, 6th Bn Connaught Rangers E. transferred from 277th Area Employment (Coy) Coy 19th Corps for me recently authorized war Grades. Auth: A.G.'s letter S.D./670 (1) of 28.1.19. —	

D.A.D.O.S. XV DIV.

CONFIDENTIAL.

WAR DIARY

D.A.D.O.S., 15th DIVISION.

March, 1919.

Army Form C. 2118

WAR DIARY
or
INTELLIGENCE SUMMARY

(Erase heading not required.)   DA D.O.S Division   March 1919

Instructions regarding War Diaries and Intelligence Summaries are contained in F. S. Regs, Part II. and the Staff Manual respectively. Title Pages will be prepared in manuscript.

Place	Date	Hour	Summary of Events and Information	Remarks and references to Appendices
Brain-Le-Chateau	1/3/19		No. 0/1002 Pte. E. Hookway. R.A.O.C. joined for duty from Base.	
—	2/3/19		(1 W.O. 3 O.Rs: to III Corps troops to form personnel of I.O.S. 15th Div & 3rd C.T.S	
			No A/1562 Armr. Sgt. D Ridding RAOC left for U.K for demobilization	
—	2/3/19		No. A/1448 Armr. Sgt. W.R. Littley RAOC left for UK for demobilization	
			Lieut Southern RAOC Asst Inspector of Arms arrived for inspection of Arms of 15th Division.	
			Capt Green D'Aufrain J.T. 6th Bn. Connaught Rangers left for duty with D.A.D.O.S 55th Division.	
			10th Scottish Rifles transferred to 33rd Division	
CLABECQ	—		1/6th A&S Highrs transferred to 33rd.	
BRAIN-LE COMTE	—			

D.A.D.O.S. 15th DIVISION.

D.A.D.O.S XV Divn

D.A.D.O.S 15th Division
War Diary for March 1919

CONFIDENTIAL.

WAR DIARY

D.A.D.O.S., 15th DIVISION.

April, 1919.

Sheets 2/1

Army Form C. 2118.

WAR DIARY
or
INTELLIGENCE SUMMARY
(Erase heading not required.)

D.A.D.O.S. 15th Divn. April 1919

Place	Date	Hour	Summary of Events and Information	Remarks and references to Appendices
Braine le Château	2/4/19		Motor Ordnance Office & Stores to Clabecq. T/Major C.M. ARCHER, R.A.O.C. arrived for duty as D.A.D.O.S.	
Braine le Comte	3/4/19		Inspection of equipment of 6th Cameron Highrs. A.F. G. 1098 signed by C.O. & Inspecting Officer.	
do.	8/4/19		do. 13th Royal Scots. do. do.	
do.	11/4/19		do. 8th Seaforth Highrs. do. do.	
TUBIZE	16/4/19		do. {4/5 Black Watch} do. do. {7/8 K.O.S.B. 9th Royal Scots} {45th & 46th High Trench Mortar Bty}	
Clabecq	17/4/19		On instructions from A.D.O.S. III Corps packet, moved Ordnance Office & Stores to H.Q. III Corps packet.	
Tubize	22/4/19		Inspection of equipment of 9th Gordon Highrs. A.F.G. 1098 signed by C.O. & Inspecting Officer.	
Hal	24/4/19		Staff Capt. T.M. Brigs. III Corps Troops:- Nos 90 & 13 Ord. Mob. Workshop, Right & No 13 Ord. Mob. Workshop, Med., Nos 10, 36 & 89 Ord. Ammun. Section, H.Q. No 38 Ration group & 52, 140, 143, 147, 179 & 186 Ration Coys.	
do.	25/4/19		02105 Thomas, T/2nd Corpl. A.S., R.A.O.C. left for U.K. for demobilization.	
do.	26/4/19		Following units arrived from O.O. III Corps Troops:- 22 Motor Amb. Convoy, 338 Roads Const. Coy. R.E. & 31, 139 & 213 P. of W. Coys.	
—	28/4/19		Equipment of following units inspected and A.F. G. 1098 signed by	

WAR DIARY
INTELLIGENCE SUMMARY.
(Erase heading not required.)

Army Form C. 2118.

Sheets 2/2

Place	Date	Hour	Summary of Events and Information	Remarks and references to Appendices
H.A.L.	29/5		C.O.'s Inspecting Officer :- No 6 & 7 Field Ambulances, H.Q. 15th Divnl. R.E. 67, 73 & 91 Field Coys. R.E. Equipment of No 5 Field Amb. inspected & A.F.G. 1098 prepared. Moved 1/22 Reserve & No 10 Ord. Amm. Sectn. to D.A.D.O.S. 8th Divn.	
	30/5		Equipment & following units, inspected and A.F.G. 1098 prepared by C.O.'s Inspecting Officer :- H.Q. 71 Bde. D.A. and "A","C" & "D" Batteries, H.Q. 158 Army Bde. R.F.A. and "A","B","C" & "D" Batteries & Bde. Amm. Col.	

C. J. Ashton
Major R.A.O.C.
D.A.D.O.S. 15th Divn.
1/5/'19

Army Form C. 2118.

WAR DIARY
or
INTELLIGENCE SUMMARY
(Erase heading not required.)

D.A.D.O.S. 15th Division May 1919

WD 47

Place	Date	Hour	Summary of Events and Information	Remarks and references to Appendices
Atl	1/5/19		Inspection of Equipment of 74th Field Coy. R.E. AFG 1098 signed by E.O. and Inspecting Officer	
"	2/5/19		Equipment of following Units inspected and AFG 1098 signed by E.O. and Inspecting Officer :- 49th Bde. Signal Sub. Section R.G.A. - 99th & 166th Siege Bty. R.G.A.	
"	3/5/19		Equipment of following Units inspected and AFG 1098 signed by E.O. and Inspecting Officer :- H.Q. 43rd Bde. R.G.A. - Signal Sub. Section 43rd Bde. R.G.A. - 61st, 100th, 102nd, 346th, 147th, 526th, 351st & 190th Siege Btys. R.G.A.	
"	6/5/19		Equipment of following Units inspected and AFG 1098 signed by C/o and Inspecting Officer :- 21st Heavy Bty. R.G.A. - Nos 9 & 13 Ord. Mobile Workshops (Right) & No.13 Ord Mobile Workshops (Medium)	
"	7/5/19		Following Unit arrived from O.O. 19th Corps Troops No1 :- 4th Middlesex Labour Coy. Equipment of following Units inspected and AFG 1098 signed by C/o and Inspecting Officer :- H.Q. 444th Infy Bde & H.Q. 45th Infy Bde.	
"	8/5/19		Inspection of Equipment of 64th Bde Signal Sub Section R.G.A. AFG 1098 signed by E.O. and Inspecting Officer. 0/3454 Pte Luscombe B. & 0/17774 Pte Watkins B. R.A.O.C. left for U.K. for	

WAR DIARY or INTELLIGENCE SUMMARY

Army Form C. 2118.

(Erase heading not required.) D.A.D.O.S. 15th Division.   May 1919

Place	Date	Hour	Summary of Events and Information	Remarks and references to Appendices
Ital.	8/5/19		Demobilization. 45th Black Watch Cadre to U.K. A/70 Bde R.F.A. trans.	
"	9/5/19		Joined to U.K.	
"	10/5/19		Inspection of Equipment of 46th Infy Bde H.Q. A.F.G.1098 signed by C.O. and Inspecting Officer	
"	11/5/19		" 101st Siege Bty. R.G.A. "	
"	12/5/19		" B/71st Bde R.F.A. "	
"	13/5/19		" "	Major Simpson
"	14/5/19		Equipment of following Units inspected and AFG 1098 signed by C.O's and Inspecting Officers:- Nos 1 & 2 Sections 15th D.A.C. & S.A.A. Section.	15th Divison
"	15/5/19		Equipment of following Units inspected and AFG 1098 signed by C.O's and Inspecting Officer:- 71st Bde R.F.A. Signal Sub Section & 15th Div. Signal M.T. Section	O & A
"	16/5/19		Equipment of following Units inspected and AFG 1098 signed by C.O's and Inspecting Officer:- H.Q. 15th D.A.C. - 15th Div H.Q. - 15th Signal Coy. R.E. - 216th Employment Coy & X & Y/15th T.M.B.	D & A
"	17/5/19		143rd Labour Coy disbanded.	
"	20/5/19		2499 L/Cpl Moness P.E. left for U.K. for demobilization. 4186 Cpl Mather A.S. & 351775 Pte Fraser W.S. 19th Royal Scots & 314482 L/Cpl Ross J. 61975 Pte Jackson J.	
"	29/5/19		& 59519 Pte Paul A. 13th Royal Scots joined for instruction under G.R.O. 6538.	

Army Form C. 2118.

WAR DIARY
or
INTELLIGENCE SUMMARY
(Erase heading not required.)   D.A.D.O.S. 15th. DIVISION.   MAY 1919.

Place	Date	Hour	Summary of Events and Information	Remarks and references to Appendices
HAL	3/6/19		S/3991 T/Sub.Cdr. Wheeler, J.E. R.A.O.C. awarded the M.S.M. Authority : London Gazette d/3/6/19.	
	5/6/19		O/1002 Pte. Hookway, E. R.A.O.C. left for U.K. for demobilization. No. 351481 Cpl. Allen, J.L., 1/9th., Royal Scots, joined for duty under G.R.O. 6538. Moved the following Units from D.A.D.O.S. 15th., Division to D.A.D.O.S. A&H Sub-AREA,: H.Q. 38th., Labour Group, 137th., P.O.W. Company, and 89th., Ord., Ammunition Section.	
	7/6/19		Inspection of Equipment of 286 Siege Btty. R.G.A. AFG.1098 signed by C.O. and Inspecting Officer.	
	8/6/19		No. 295510 Pte. Hurford, E.J. 12th., Somerset Light Infantry & No. 57518 Pte.Brophy, G.W. 24th., Welsh Regt., joined for duty from D.A.D.O.S. 74th., Division.	
	12/6/19		Stores handed in of H.Q. & No. 1 Coy.15th. Divnl. Train. Units not yet disbanded.	
	13/6/19		" " " " 2 " " " "	
	16/6/19		" " " " 3 " " " "	
	17/6/19		H.Q.70th. Bde. R.F.A., B,C,&D,Bttys. & Signal Sub-Section 70th. Bde. R.F.A. transferred to U.K. Stores handed in of No.4 Coy. Train. Unit not yet disbanded. Inspection of Equipment of 215 A.T. Coy. R.E. AFG.1098 signed by C.O. and Inspecting Officer. Cadres of the following Units to U.K. H.Q.15th. D.A.C. Nos.1,2, & S.A.A.Sections D.A.C. X&Y/15 Med. Trench Mortar Battery.	
	18/6/19		Cadres of the following Units to U.K. A,B,& C, Bttys. 71st. Bde. R.F.A.	
	19/6/19		" " " " " " 9th.& 13th. Ord.Mob.Workshops (Light). 13th. Ord.Mob. Workshops (Medium). Inspection of Equipment of 217 Siege Btty. R.G.A. AFG 1098 signed by C.O. and Inspecting Officer. No. O/4609 Sgt. VERE, B. R.A.O.C. left for U.K. for demobilization.	
	20/6/19		Cadres of the following Units to U.K. H.Q.71st. Bde. R.F.A. D,Btty. & Signal Sub-Section 71st. Bde. R.F.A. 9th. Gordon Hdrs. 45th. Field Ambulance.	
	21/6/19		Following Units disbanded. H.Q.15th. Div. R.A. 153th. Bde. A.F.A. Ammn. Column. "Fourchange" Animal Staging Camp, Nivelles. Anstag, O. Cadres of the following Units to U.K. A,B,& C,Bttys. 153th. Bde. A.F.A.	
	22/6/19		Cadres of the following Units to U.K. H.Q.158th. Bde. A.F.A. D,Btty.158th. Bde. A.F.A. 46th. Field Ambulance.	
	23/6/19		" " " " " 8th. Seaforth Hdrs. 6th. Cameron Hdrs. 44th. Infy. Bde.H.Q. 44th. Light Trench Mortar Battery. 47th. Field Ambulance.	
	24/6/19		" " " " " 27th. Mob. Vety. Section. 7/8th. K.O.S.B. 1/9th. Royal Scots. 74th. Field Coy. R.E. Inspection of Equipment of 1/1st. Northumberland Hussars. AFG1098 signed by C.O. and Inspecting Officer.	
	25/6/19		Inspection of Equipment of 237th. 323rd. & 119th. Siege Bttys. R.G.A. AFG 1098 signed by C.O. and Inspecting Officer.	

Army Form C. 2118.

WAR DIARY
or ~~INTELLIGENCE SUMMARY~~

(Erase heading not required.) D.A.D.O.S. 15th. DIVISION. MAY 1919.

Instructions regarding War Diaries and Intelligence Summaries are contained in F. S. Regs., Part II. and the Staff Manual respectively. Title pages will be prepared in manuscript.

Place	Date	Hour	Summary of Events and Information	Remarks and references to Appendices
HAL.	25/6/19		Cadres of the following Units to U.K. H.Q.45th. Infy. Bde. 45th. Light Trench Mortar Btty. 73rd.& 91st. Field Coys. R.E. 13th. Royal Scots. 155th. Bde. A.F.A.Signal Sub-Section disbanded.	
	26/6/19		Inspection of Equipment of H.Q.III Corps H.A. AFG 1098 signed by C.O. and Inspecting Officer.	
	27/6/19		" " " " H.Q.III Corps ~~A.E.Coy.~~ B " " " "	
			No. O/7182 Pte. Worthington, J. A.O.C. left for U.K. for demobilization.	

3rd. July 1919.

Carter Major,
D.A.D.O.S. 15th. Division.

www.ingramcontent.com/pod-product-compliance
Lightning Source LLC
Chambersburg PA
CBHW081427160426
43193CB00013B/2215